R C Wolfe
from Susan

Modern
Fly Dressings for the
Practical Angler

POUL JORGENSEN

Modern Fly Dressings for the Practical Angler

Photographs by the author
Introduction by Lefty Kreh
Preface by Art Lee

Winchester Press

Second printing   1976

WINCHESTER is a Trademark of Olin Corporation
used by Winchester Press, Inc. under authority
and control of the Trademark Proprietor.

Copyright © 1976 by Poul Jorgensen
All rights reserved
Library of Congress Catalog Card Number: 76-2060
Library of Congress Cataloging in Publication Data
Jorgensen, Poul.
Modern fly dressings for the practical angler.
Includes index.
1. Fly tying.   2. Flies, Artificial.   I. Title.
SH451.J64   688.7'9   76-2060
ISBN 0-87691-224-2
Published by Winchester Press
205 East 42nd Street, New York 10017
Printed in the United States of America

To those who live and fish by the Creed of the Brotherhood of the Jungle Cock, I proudly dedicate this book.

CREED

We, who love angling, in order that it may enjoy practice and reward in the later generations, mutually move together toward a common goal—the conservation and restoration of American game fishes.

Towards this end we pledge that our creel limits shall always be less than the legal restrictions and always well within the bounty of Nature herself.

Enjoying, as we do, only a life estate in the out of doors, and morally charged in our time with the responsibility of handing it down unspoiled to tomorrow's inheritors, we individually undertake annually to take at least one boy a-fishing, instructing him, as best we know, in the responsibilities that are soon to be wholly his.

Holding that moral law transcends the legal statutes, always beyond the needs of any one man, and holding that example alone is the one certain teacher, we pledge always to conduct ourselves in such fashion on the stream as to make safe for others the heritage which is ours and theirs.

Contents

Introduction by Lefty Kreh   ix

Preface by Art Lee   xi

Acknowledgments   xv

1. Insects and Their Importance in Fly-Fishing   3

2. Hooks and Tools   9

3. Materials   21
   BASIC MATERIALS   22
   HACKLE   29
   FUR   30
   LATEX   36
   SUPPLIERS OF FLY-TYING MATERIALS   36

4. Mayfly Nymphs   39
   TYPES OF NATURAL MAYFLY NYMPHS   39
   DRESSING THE MAYFLY NYMPH, STEP BY STEP   43

SELECTED NYMPH AND IMPORTANT EMERGER AND
WET-FLY DRESSINGS   55
CRUSTACEANS   66

5. Mayfly Duns and Spinners   69
    DRESSING THE MAYFLY DUN, STEP BY STEP   70
    DRESSING THE MAYFLY SPINNER, STEP BY STEP   88
    SELECTED MAYFLY DUN AND SPINNER DRESSINGS   98

6. Caddis Flies   119
    DRESSING THE CADDIS LARVA, STEP BY STEP   121
    DRESSING THE CADDIS PUPA, STEP BY STEP   129
    DRESSING THE CADDIS ADULT, STEP BY STEP   143

7. Stone Fly Nymphs   159
    DRESSING THE STONE FLY NYMPH, STEP BY STEP   162
    SELECTED STONE FLY NYMPH DRESSINGS   176

8. Terrestrial Insects   183
    BEETLES   183
    CRICKETS AND GRASSHOPPERS   191
    RED AND BLACK ANTS   196

9. Hellgrammite Larvae   201

    Index   221

Introduction

by Lefty Kreh

Make no mistake, this is a *new* fly-tying book. In it Poul Jorgensen has described many of the latest techniques of the art of tying flies, and unlike many recent publications that merely rehash traditional methods, it is truly novel as well as practical.

Poul's last book, *Dressing Flies for Fresh and Salt Water,* is a superb piece of work. This book is built upon that base, but gives up-to-date dope. Even if you're a novice, I believe you'll find the tricks of a top professional interesting to you and useful in your own fly-fishing.

This is not a "bug" book. Poul has deliberately leaned away from making it a complicated monograph that could be understood only by those with a background in science. Instead, while scientific names are given for the flies, the descriptions, common names, and other information are all at the level that fishermen can understand and work with.

Poul's introduction to the general fly-tying public of Raleigh Boaze's method of using latex material for nymphs, and Poul's own innovations with this interesting new material, will fascinate you—and help you tie better nymphs.

I have tied and fished with many of Poul's all-fur nymphs, and I rate them about as deadly for all-round use as any nymphs I ever drifted through a pool—East or West.

Poul passes on his experiences with a new dubbing material that looks like seal's fur, acts like seal's fur, and works like seal's fur—but is not. Yet, fish take it for the real thing.

Poul has for the first time given formulas for mixing furs to get the desired shades. Marking pens have been an inside secret with many of us who tie a great deal. But Poul has simplified their use so you can get exactly the shade you want and can later duplicate it.

ix

Larry Solomon of New York City has accumulated an enormous amount of data and useful information concerning the caddis fly, and he has generously allowed Poul to use this material in the book. As most good trout fishermen know, the caddis is one of the most important foods for trout, and this totally new treatment of this important classification of insects will enhance any trout fisherman's ability to tie better flies—and catch more fish.

—LEFTY KREH

Cockeysville, Maryland

Preface

by Art Lee

Fly-tying is an evolving art that probably couldn't quit even if it wanted to. There is too much momentum, too much inertia, too many inquisitive minds, too many fish that plain won't take. Which is the way it always was and hopefully always will be. If we fly-fishermen and fly-tyers once for a moment thought we had the problem licked, that we had discovered the ultimate answer, all that we would be doing is proving that, as Lavater wrote, "He whose pride oppresses the humble, may, perhaps, be humbled, but will never be humble."

If you had ever advised my grandfather to try a Tricorythodes, he would have thought you were suggesting he fish with a dinosaur. Yet, today, wherever there is water and fly-fishing, you're bound to hear almost as much Latin and Greek astream as you do English. And while we're on the subject of Greek, which brings to mind

antiquity, let me mention that I don't for an instant credit any ancient Greek with first affixing feathers to a hook to catch fish. That would be to accept a prescribed beginning for fly-fishing that while tidy enough for the historian, is both unfitting and unnecessary for the angler truly sensitive to the subject. I would prefer to believe that some ancestor much farther removed in time found a fish he couldn't catch, cut some of his copious forearm hair, wound it around a sharpened piece of bone, and WHAMMO.

Now, that is not to say that the contribution of a certain old Roman (who was, I believe, called Sparsehaccullus Greius, although several volumes of his work under that *nom de plume* were apparently lost when his wife learned how he was spending his spare time) is not important to fly-tying's evolution. If he had wasted time building wooden horses or writing odes instead of doing something really important, there is no telling how long fishermen might have waited before somebody gave Cotton and Walton, Halford, Skues, and Gordon the news. Besides, if somebody has to get the credit, it's better in the face of current world affairs to have it go to an ancient Roman than to an Egyptian pharaoh. And, if the angler had had to wait until another fair child of grace saw fit to go into a convent on the banks of a trout stream to get the whole thing rolling, we all might have been stuck with worms forever.

There are few fly-fishermen and fewer fly-tyers who do not know of and deeply appreciate the contributions of Dame Juliana Berners and the others of other centuries to our sport. Their works fill our library shelves. *The Compleat Angler* is still No. 2 on the all-time best seller list, I understand, outstripped only by the Bible. Certainly more fly-fishermen can quote from the Halford-Gordon letters, which smell of limestone and pine, than can mime Barrett-Browning woos which smell of lavender. That is fine, too.

The art and science of fly-tying has come a long, long way, however, and it is likely that preoccupation with the distant past dims the contemporary and clouds the future. It might be wiser to think more of those who in more recent times have done so much to bring this evolving art to its current state. We might pause to applaud Lee Wulff, who solved the problem of the fragile "fly-tyer's fly," the

fanwing, that could sustain the punishment of only one successful cast if it did not spin the tippet into a bird's nest first, with those hair-winged dry flies which bear his name and are so often taken for granted by all of us. Of Harry and Elsie Darbee and of Walt and Winnie Dette, who have carried fly-tying through the days of silk and shoemaker's wax to a degree of sophistication without compromise to quality unthought of even in the days of Theodore Gordon. Of Ernest Schwiebert, whose erudition and talent is seemingly boundless. Of Charles K. Fox and Vince Marinaro, who have refined fine-tippet fishing to a science. Of Lefty Kreh, who has carried our little wands and creations from the vise to Father Neptune and showed us they can be adapted practically. Of Art Flick, whose study and little book have done as much as anything in history to bring our sport and art to everyman. Yes, of Don Zahner, who was willing to take the great personal and financial gamble that everyman would be interested in our progress and our jottings.

But, most of all, perhaps, before we turn another page as tomorrow becomes today, we might pause to thank Bill Blades, who was a great innovator himself, and was graceful and thoughtful enough, doing the old Roman one better, not only to take the trouble to write it down but to pass along with tireless exactness his technique to the man who may just be the greatest living dresser of flies—Poul Jorgensen. We should thank Bill Blades for knowing a willing and incredibly innovative pupil when he was one, able to learn well what Bill Blades could show him, the art of tying flies, while also absorbing the critical lesson Bill Blades inspired just by the very nature of the man.

"This is a school from which you'll never graduate. When you're eighty, there'll still be too much to learn."

—Art Lee

Roscoe, N.Y. (on the Willowemoc), 1975

ACKNOWLEDGMENTS

When the long-awaited moment is before you in the form of a mountain of typewritten pages, glossy photographs, and letters from the publisher telling you that you are already late, there is a feeling of inner peace that only an author can know. It is time to think back, maybe to the days of childhood when my father took me fishing, or to the sunny afternoon on the Little Diamond Lake north of Chicago where I met the late Bill Blades, the man who started it all and taught me the difference between tying flies and just flytying.

In my modest library of books by learned authors I have yet to open one wherein it is said, "I did it all by myself," and this one is no different.

I wish to thank all the anglers and flytyers with whom I have exchanged ideas. A special note of gratitude to Raleigh Boaze, Jr., for letting me introduce latex and its various uses.

I also wish to thank Larry Solomon and Crown Publishers, who so generously let me use the caddis dry-fly patterns and share them with the rest of our fellow anglers.

A heartfelt thanks to Dr. Jim Gilford of Frederick, Maryland, for letting me use the beautiful photograph of our beloved Green Drake in its natural splendor. It is found where it belongs—on the book jacket. And to Bill Elliott for the fine drawings of insects found throughout the book. They are priceless!

I also wish to express my sincere appreciation to Art Lee, a good friend and fishing companion, for writing his preface. If nothing else is read in this book, I hope at least Art's preface is.

I would also like to extend a most heartfelt thanks to a man whose expertise is endless, my good friend Lefty Kreh, for teaching me to use the camera and standing ready to help when needed. Without his expert advice this book would have quite a few blank pages.

And last but not least, to the girl who worked tirelessly at the typewriter keyboard when we put it all together. Without her you would not read this. Thank you, Nancy.

—POUL JORGENSEN

Towson, Maryland
January 1976

Modern
Fly Dressings for the
Practical Angler

1
Insects and Their Importance in Fly-Fishing

I suppose it's reasonable to assume that in general, insects are regarded as a nuisance by humans. But most of them somehow manage to justify their existence. While the fly-fisher may not appreciate all the small creatures that cross his path, he welcomes the sight of flies swarming over his favorite trout water and bringing it to life with leaping and feeding fish. To capitalize on such ideal fishing conditions the angler must identify the insects upon which the fish are feeding and come up with a reasonable artificial.

For the novice this may sound like a mystery. A friend said to me not long ago, "All these discussions about flies, leader tippets, upstream and downstream drift, were hard enough to comprehend, but now that one must learn entomology in order to become a producer of one's own fishing flies I am beginning to think that fly-fishing is purposely made difficult and

designed for the enjoyment of a few with special talent—and so is fly-tying, for that matter." On the contrary, fly-fishing can be learned by anyone in a very short time. It is just a way of catching fish under circumstances where other methods are useless or less practical, and, of course, it is a way of enjoying oneself. The fly-tying aspect of the sport is to many much more important than fishing itself. It can be made as simple or as complicated as you want it to be. Anyone who can tie his own shoelaces can learn to tie a fishing fly, provided he is willing to practice. I have never found that I needed a college degree in entomology, and for years I have been able to get by with the knowledge gained by reading articles and books dealing with the subject, and by observing the happenings at streamsides where insects abound. The fly-fisher will soon discover that fish will feed on a juicy grasshopper as well as on a tiny midge type of insect that one can't even see. Life in or near the stream or lake covers a wide spectrum of insect species, of which only a very small group is of interest to the angler.

The principal insects dealt with in this book are mayflies, caddis flies, and stone flies. I also discuss some other less important aquatic species. Within each order of insect there are hundreds of species identified by entomologists, but recorded observations by many dedicated American anglers have narrowed the list to a very few principal hatches, in imitation of which so many fly patterns have been devised.

It is helpful to understand the life cycle of insects. The immature nymph and larva make up a large portion of the fish's diet. In fact, it is estimated that fish consume 85 percent of their food underwater, which explains why a "dry-fly purist" can often get skunked while the nympher is having good fishing. When nymphs are ready to hatch they become very active and are out of hiding in full view of the fish. Before a nymph hatches the skin splits open either underwater, on rocks, or in the surface film, and the winged adult appears. In the case of caddis and stone flies, no other transformation takes place and they are ready for mating and egglaying. But the mayfly undergoes one more change. When it first appears it is known to the angler as a dun. If it manages to escape the fish feasting on a new hatch and flies to safety, it will change

into a spinner, usually within twenty-four hours. The fly has now completely changed. The wings are in most cases glossy-clear, and the tails are much longer than those of the dun.

The ability to recognize whether the fish are feeding on the nymph underwater or the emerging nymph in the surface film, or whether they are feeding on the dun or the spinner, is very important not only to the fly-fisher, but to the fly-tyer as well. When the spinners appear over the stream or lake, the mating flight begins. The flies can usually be observed high over the water, often in large swarms. As mating progresses they fly lower and lower, and ultimately the egglaying takes place in the water. The spinners now die, thus ending the life cycle of a precious insect.

During the active period just before or during a hatch, the fish will go wild and the water is often boiling with feeding fish. In most instances the fish become very selective and will feed only on the particular fly hatching at the time. This is perhaps one of the biggest mysteries to many, as it seems quite unreasonable that a fish will refuse a big juicy fly, but be quite willing to gorge on a hatch of tiny midges.

For several years now I have collected some fly specimens every time I went fishing, and needless to say, these specimens have been invaluable as models in my fly-tying efforts. The equipment for starting a collection of insects is relatively inexpensive, or you can make it yourself.

1-1 In fast water I use a large seine of window screen to collect naturals for study. (Photo: Lefty Kreh)

For collecting underwater specimens in riffles or deep fast water, I use a home-made seine consisting of a piece of cheese-cloth or window screen suspended between two half-inch dowels. I prefer one large one approximately 3×4 feet for heavy-duty work, and one small portable seine 1×1½ feet with quarter-inch sticks and cheesecloth so that it can be rolled up and carried in the fishing vest. The seine is operated by standing in the water facing downstream and placing the seine in front of you at an arm's length. It should be spread out and held perpendicular to the stream in a vertical position with the lower edge resting firmly against the stream bottom. Now move rocks and disturb the bottom with your feet, and the nymphs and larvae will be dislodged and carried into the seine by the current. Specimens floating in the surface film can be scooped up with a small aquarium net. I capture flying specimens with a butterfly net that has been modified and fitted with a male ferrule so that it can be mounted on the butt section of my fly rod. Winged

Insects and Their Importance in Fly-Fishing
5

1-2 I carry this small cheese-cloth seine in my fishing vest. (Photo: Lefty Kreh)

1-3 An aquarium net is handy for scooping emerging naturals from the surface. (Photo: Lefty Kreh)

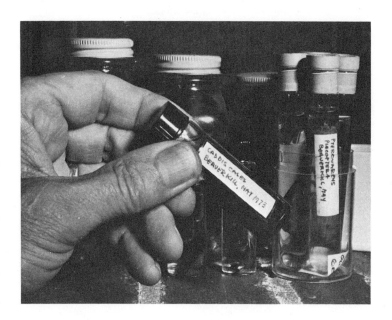

1-4 I keep my specimens in tightly corked bottles in a solution of alcohol, glycerine, and vinegar.

specimens can at times be picked up by hand or with small tweezers from their resting places on trees, bushes, and fences near the stream. Some species are attracted by light from a lantern or automobile in the evening, although it is always best to do the collecting when a hatch is on to assure yourself of getting the right specimens. Since our specimens are to be used as models for the dressing of artificial fishing flies and not for further entomological study, I am satisfied by taking some notes about the color and other characteristics that might be helpful when trying to make positive identification after returning home.

I have talked to many who, like myself, collect a few insects every time they go fishing, and most of us agree that although we have neither the time nor the ambition to become entomologists, it is extremely important to have a collection of basic insect types for use as models in our tying efforts. Not all my fishing friends keep the insects; some merely take notes right at streamside, such as the insect's size, color, and dominating features, which will be helpful to them at a later date. It is best, however, to preserve some specimens in addition to the notes one takes on the spot. Since it is not very practical to pin the insects on a board in a dried version because they will eventually deteriorate, I keep them in small glass containers sealed with a tightly fitted cork. Specimens should be kept separate from each other, and there should be no more than a few of the same species together.

There are many different preserving solutions, and I have tried most of them. I presently use a solution consisting of eight parts grain alcohol, one part vinegar, and one part glycerine to prevent the insect from becoming too brittle to handle. Many simply use straight alcohol of 70 to 80 percent strength. Before storing the prepared specimens I label the glass container with the name and where and when it was collected. Some specimens are merely given a number and information pertaining to the specimen is kept on a separate card.

2
Hooks and Tools

Hook Specifications

Regardless of the brand of equipment that you have chosen for your fly-fishing, it is the hook that you ultimately must rely upon when the fish is hooked and being played. The best recommendation anyone can give is to use only the very finest fly-tying hooks.

I have systematically discarded inferior hooks that I bought from time to time either because I ran out of my regular brand or because my supplier was out of a particular type that I needed. In any event, they were discarded for various reasons. First of all, fly-tying hooks have character. Maybe you don't believe it, but nevertheless they do. Since I try to select the hook that is best suited for a particular artificial, I want to be able to choose the length of the shank so that it will accommodate the body of the insect I am copy-

ing and at the same time end up with a hook gap that will not be a dead giveaway and yet will be large enough to accommodate the fish being sought.

In the case of dry-fly hooks there is little choice in combinations of shank length and hook gap unless one is willing to choose a heavier-than-normal hook, or one with an extremely short shank, such as is often used for dressing the traditional spider-type dry flies. With subsurface hooks, it is different. There we have a large number of combinations from which to choose, and with experience you will soon discover that even when you have the best hooks in the world, you as the fly-tyer must select the ones with characteristics best suited for the insects you copy.

For years I was thoroughly convinced that the only types of hooks worthy of use for dressing the subaquatic artificials were

16

14

12

10

8

6

16

14

12

10

8

6

4

2

2-1 *Left.*
Mustad #3906
and #3906B, in
Size 6 to 16.

2-2 *Right.*
Mustad #38941,
3X Long, in Size
2 to 16.

2-3 Mustad
#3665A, 6X
Long, in Size 1
to 8.

8

6

4

2

1

those with a perfectly round bend, and would probably have gone on believing this had it not been for someone who pointed out to me that while he thought my nymphs were as good as the rest of them, they would frequently ride upside down in the water—a disadvantage, he thought. In experimenting with other hook forms I came to think of a discussion I once had with Harry Darbee, the famous Catskill fly-dresser and a knowledgeable salmon angler. He mentioned that he never fully understood why saltwater flies were not dressed on salmon hooks so that they would ride right side up. Then I remembered that most salmon flies do ride right side up, a condition attributed mostly to the shape of the hook bend, which is a Limerick, very much like the Sproat bend on a good many wet-fly hooks. (Incidentally, most saltwater flies are now tied on hooks with Sproat or Limerick bend.) I have dressed my nymphs on Sproat-bend hooks since and eliminated the upside-down problem in most cases.

WET-FLY AND NYMPH HOOKS

MUSTAD #3906: Turned-down eye, bronzed, with a Sproat bend. It is considered a regular-length hook which I use primarily for caddis larvae and pupae, but it can, of course, be used to dress other types as well.

MUSTAD #3906B: This is the same type of hook with the same specifications, except that the shank is extra long, which is usually designated as being 1X Long. While this hook can be used for the dressing of caddis pupae, I have selected it primarily for nymphs, and the extra length and Sproat bend make it unbeatable for medium-size dressings.

MUSTAD #38941: Like the #3906 and #3906B, this hook has a turned-down eye and a Sproat bend, but the shank is 3X Long and chosen to accommodate some of the larger nymphs of both mayflies and stone flies.

2-4 Mustad
#94833, 3X
Fine, in Size 6 to
22.

14

12

10

8

6

22

20

18

16

2-5 Mustad
#94842, in Size
8 to 26.

26

24

22

20

18

16

14

12

10

8

MUSTAD #3665A: This hook has a turned-down eye and a Limerick bend. The 6X Long shank lends itself well for dressing the large subaquatic insects such as hellgrammites and fishfly larvae.

DRY-FLY HOOKS

The two types of hooks I always use for my dry flies are Mustad #94833 and #94842. The first, #94833, is a regular dry-fly hook with turned-down eye and a round bend. The wire from which it is made is 3X Fine. It is a good all-round dry-fly hook for artificials designed to float on their hackle, such as the caddis dry fly. The very small sizes are also used for some miniature nymphs in cases where the somewhat heavier wire of a wet-fly hook is not practical because of size.

Mustad #94842 is slightly different. It has a turned-up eye and is made from extra-fine wire. The turned-up eye is im-

portant for dressing the artificials that float with the aid of their fur body, such as all the spinners and parachute duns. If the eye penetrates or lies in the surface film, it generates a very distorted view of the fly when seen from underwater.

ORDERING HOOKS

The hooks I have described are those I have found to be most suitable for the flies in this book, but that is not to say that others could not be used if they fit the specifics outlined in the text. And, of course, I use many other types of hooks for some of the many artificial flies of importance.

As a general rule it is sufficient to mention the brand name, in this case Mustad, in addition to the quality number and hook size. When ordering hooks from your supplier it is more economical to buy them in boxes of 100; the savings over buying them in packages of 25 or less are considerable. To permit fishing different streams and now and then taking a trip to an unknown area, I recommend the purchase of a full range of hook sizes to avoid the frustration of being in the right place at the right time but with the wrong size flies.

Since I think it is important for the fly-tyer to take advantage of the varied characteristics of hooks so that he can get the best overall proportions for his artificials—that is, proper length, weight, hook gap, etc.—I would like to explain the meaning of the "X" so frequently associated with the description of the hooks. Each hook manufacturer has a standard (or regular) length of each size hook he makes. Standard hooks have a certain size gap and wire diameter which gradually gets smaller as the hooks get smaller. Any deviation from the standard length within a particular hook size is called 1X, 2X, 3X, 4X, etc., up to 6X Long. If the hook specification reads "Mustad #3906B 1X Long," the length of the shank is equal to that of a regular (in this case #3906) hook one size larger, but the hook gap and wire diameter remain unchanged.

The same graduating scale is used when determining the wire diameter. Thus if a dry-fly hook is designated "3X Fine," it simply means that the wire used in its manufacture is the same as that used for a regular hook three sizes smaller.

Even though manufacturers of hooks have very rigid standards in quality control throughout the entire hookmaking process, the majority of hooks are not as sharp as they should be, and I recommend that they be sharpened with a small stone or file before being used.

Tools

Some years ago I wrote a short article, "Reconstruction of Historic American Trout Flies," for *The American Fly Fisher*, a publication sponsored by the Museum of American Fly Fishing, of which I am a trustee and adviser. While doing research I came across an article dealing with a method of making artificial flies published in the *American Turf Register* in September 1830. The nameless author describes his method of dressing the fly by holding the hook firmly between the first finger and thumb on the left hand, with the bend toward the base of the fingers and the barb downward. He continues to explain how the entire fly is dressed, including the snell, by holding the hook in the fingers and aided by no other tools than a pair of fine-pointed scissors. This is doing it the hard way, and unless you try it yourself some day, you may never really appreciate your vise and other accessories.

Nevertheless, I have long been an advocate of using as few tools as is practical, stressing the importance of training your fingers to do the job of the many "gadgets" offered for sale by suppliers. Instead, one might do well by investing in a

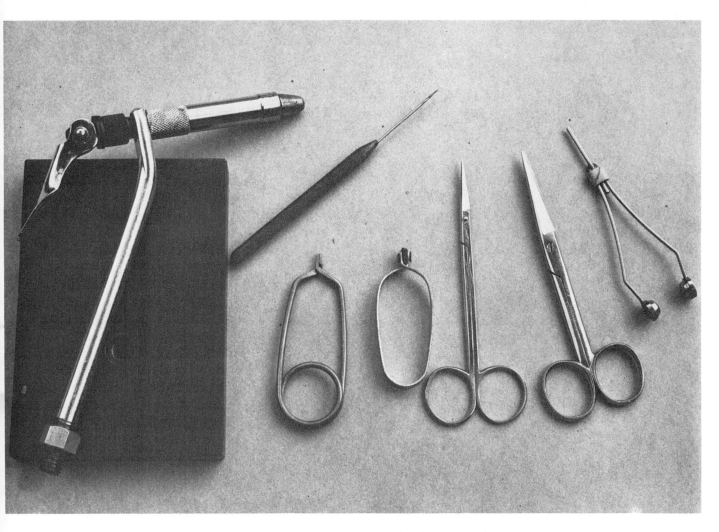

2-6 Basic fly-dressing tools.

really good vise and a pair or two of fine scissors. The basic tools of a fly-dresser are shown in Fig. 2-6, but in addition, there are a few things I have found practical to use for various special techniques found throughout the book.

HACKLE GAUGE

Being able to select the right size hackle for your dry flies is pretty important, and unless you have a lot of experience and can pick them from the cape and estimate their size at a glance, you will need a small hackle gauge.

The one I use is a homemade affair consisting of a thin piece of aluminum sheet,

1×4 inches. One end is tapered so that it will fit in the jaws of the vise, and on the other end is a small spur that serves as a guiding post for the hackle stem. The measuring scale is a small piece of cardboard glued to the aluminum with the lower edge snug up against the guidepost. To make the fiber-length guidelines on the board, lay the hook on the cardboard with the shank against the guidepost and make a mark on the card at a position equal to $1\frac{1}{2}$ to 2 times the hook gap, measuring from the guidepost. Now draw a line across the board, making sure to leave enough room at one end for the hook-size number. Make several such lines by using the various size hooks used most often for dressing your flies. You

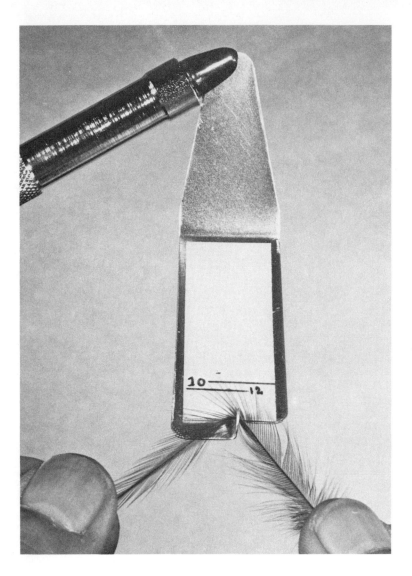

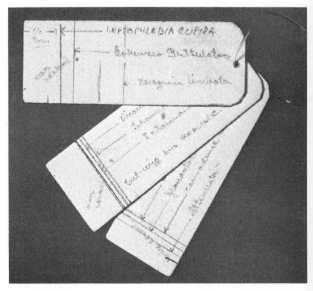

2-7 Homemade hackle gauge. Here it is held in the vise jaws; it can also be held at table level by the vise clamp.

2-8 I find these measuring cards a great convenience for cut-wing patterns.

can bend the aluminum forward toward you after it is placed in the vise to get a comfortable work angle.

To use the gauge, hold the hackle by each end and lay it on the board with the middle portion of the stem against the guidepost. Pull the hackle ends lightly toward you as seen in Fig. 2-7 and the fibers will angle up on the board so the length can be determined.

MEASURING CARDS

Since I often use fly wings that are cut from whole feathers, I made a set of cards with the different wing lengths marked off with a pencil line across a small $1^1/_2 \times 3$-inch piece of cardboard. The wing lengths are set off from the narrow edge of the card and identified by the name of the fly for which it is used. Lay the feather on the board and line the lower fibers up with the pencil line. Trim the excess feather along the cardboard edge and you have the proper wing length. See Fig. 2-8.

CALIPER

A small caliper marked with both millimeters and inches is a helpful tool when working with artificials that require exact-

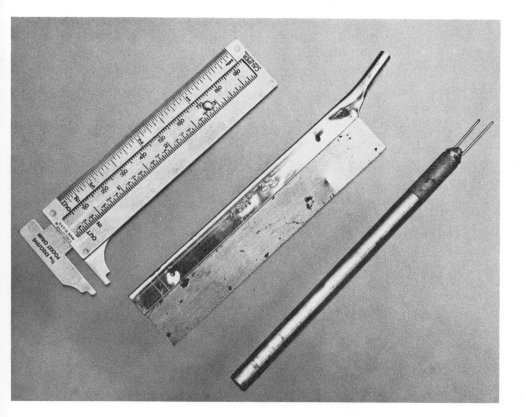

2-9 Caliper, X-Acto saw, and quill section equalizer made from X-Acto handle and a bent paper clip.

ness in proportion. They can be purchased in many sizes, but I like the small ones that take up less space on the table.

SMALL FUNNEL

To align the hair after it is cut from the skin, you can hardly beat a small funnel with a container in which it can be shook and rattled around until the hair is even. When ready, the hairs can be pushed through the narrow end where you can grasp them before they get disarranged. This setup is not found in the catalogue from Abercrombie and Fitch, but your local dime store carries funnels in various sizes, and the base can be a glass, cup, or other common object found around most households. My funnel is shown in action in the section on tying caddis adults.

QUILL SECTION EQUALIZER

This tool is designed to enable the fly-dresser to cut two wing quill sections that are exactly the same size. It is not available commercially as a unit but can be made very easily by trimming a paper clip to form the legs and inserting the piece in the end of an X-Acto knife handle. The longer leg will serve as a guide held along

Hooks and
Tools
15

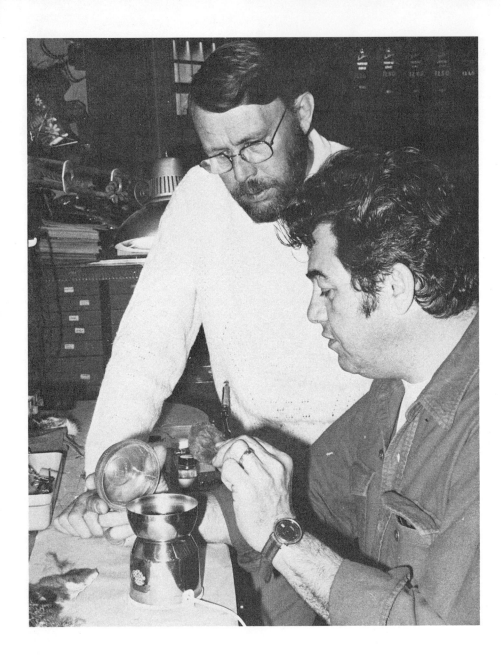

2-10 Tony Marasco blends fur in a small electric coffee grinder. (Photo: Lefty Kreh)

the edge of the quill fibers, while the other is inserted in the wing quill and drawn out through the feather, separating a particular width of quill section. The legs can be adjusted in or out, depending on the size wings you are making.

FUR BLENDER

It may seem like a luxury to buy a special piece of machinery to blend fur unless you need a lot of it, but believe me, it is the best investment you can make next to the vise. The small electric grinders used in Europe for grinding coffee beans are excellent for fur blending, as was first discovered by an Italian fly-tyer from Pittsburgh named Tony Marasco (Fig. 2-10). With a small blender you can mix fur in just seconds, and chop wool and other yarns that are so hard to pull apart.

X-ACTO SAW

This tool is rarely used in fly-tying unless you make bass bugs, but I have found it extremely useful for roughing up the dubbing when dressing the special nymphs in this book. They come in different sizes which can all be used provided they are the fine-toothed variety. Shortly after giving a demonstration of this type of dubbing at a club meeting I saw someone use a hacksaw blade, but they are too rough, particularly for making smaller nymphs.

TOENAIL CLIPPERS
(Wing Cutters)

I have seen a number of different wing cutters in action, but none can beat an ordinary pair of large toenail clippers. Dr. Scholl's "Nail Clip" is very good and can be purchased at almost any drugstore. I should like to emphasize the importance of getting one that will make a clean cut without tearing the fibers on the feather. I had to purchase four or five before finding one that did the job and would cut a perfect curve. Needless to say, such "rare tools" must be kept in the safe when not in use, or worn around the neck on a string like a medallion.

STREAMSIDE TYING KIT

I can't even begin to explain how important this little jewel has been to me over the years. A real lifesaver! After I wrote an article about it in *Trout Magazine* it was suggested that I market it for the benefit

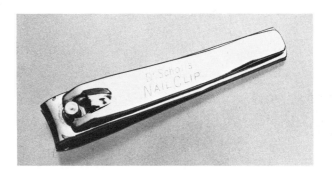

2-11 A good pair of toenail clippers will cut feathers cleanly.

2-12 My Streamside Kit.

of my fellow anglers, which has since been done. It can be purchased from Fly Fisherman's Bookcase Tackle Service, Route 9A, Croton-on-Hudson, N.Y. 10520. It is supplied with tools, including a Croydon vise, and mounting bracket, plus half a dozen fur selections and tying thread. A small brochure explains how to pack it and what essential materials to carry on the stream.

2-13 I match the hatch with a Streamside Kit while Charles K. Fox and Ross Trimmer look on. (Photo: Lefty Kreh)

3
Materials

The subject of materials has always been a confusing one, at least for someone who is just starting to tie his own flies. I am often asked if there isn't some sort of kit one can buy that has everything in it so we could eliminate all the fussing around looking for the stuff only to end up with a whole room full of more or less useless material. Unfortunately, there is no such kit, and if there were one you would have to stand in line for a long time to get one.

I clearly remember the two items I first owned when I started tying my own flies back in the mid-1950s: a brown rooster neck and razor blade, both given to me by my friend the late Bill Blades. "In case you are wondering what the razor blade is for, I'll tell you," he said while he was looking around on his little tying stand located next to a row of bridge tables full of bottles with lacquer and specimens of insects. "This hook here goes with it, and

every time the stuff you put on the hook is not to my liking, the razor blade goes into action." He was not kidding, nor was he kidding about the penny he asked for for the hook, a superstitious habit of his. Even though Bill had just moved his tying room from one bedroom to a larger one and had closets full of boxes with material, he still insisted that it's not a lot of material that makes a good fly-tyer—it's practice!

As I look around in my own tying room I wonder if I forgot to take his advice. However, most of us who have enjoyed the art of fly-tying for a number of years know that Bill's reasoning was sound and we have weeded out the unnecessary in favor of just those items which are best suited for the flies we enjoy and will take the most fish.

You will probably find the materials I discuss somewhat strange in comparison with what you are used to, and probably most of the stuff you are acquainted with is not mentioned. Instead, this chapter introduces you to a whole lot of new materials, some formerly thought of as unusable surplus and others that are brand new but particularly adaptable to the flies in this book. For those who wish to study the whole spectrum of fly-tying material, I can highly recommend a recent book written by Eric Leiser, *Fly-Tying Materials, Their Procurement, Use and Protection* (Crown Publishers, New York, 1973).

BASIC MATERIALS
THREAD

Every fly-tying bench has some basic items that are used all the time regardless of what kind of artificials you are dressing. The first that comes to my mind is tying thread, and but a few years ago it was silk, which the tyer had to wax and handle with care so as not to fray or break it. Although some of the old-timers still use it, the much stronger prewaxed nylon has become so popular that silk is hard to obtain in some areas. I have used Herb Howard's prewaxed 6/0 thread for some years now and, frankly speaking, I wouldn't know what to do without it since it is all I ever use. It comes in many different colors; if you are a serious fly-tyer, your bench should never be without black, white, brown, olive, cream, gray, yellow, and orange.

ADDITIONAL WAX

I still have a lump of special wax that was given to me by Bill Blades, and which sits in the end of an empty wooden thread spool. His recipe was as complicated as the one he used for his basement wine-making and was extremely sticky, which in the days of unwaxed thread was a blessing. Wax is now readily available from your supplier in small pieces and is used for "extra waxing" the thread if needed. I rarely use it except to rub on my fingertips when they get too dry for comfortable working.

CEMENT

There are many different brands of head cement you can get from a supplier, each claiming to be better than the other. For applying on the hook before winding a dubbing, or for finishing heads on nymphs and dry flies, I have found none better than clear nail polish, which in case you didn't know is merely a high-grade lacquer that happens also to be a good binding agent for various parts of a fishing fly.

SILICONE GLUE

When I first started to make the extension bodies for realistic-type mayflies, they were awkward, clumsy, and heavy because of the material from which they were made. But since I started to use the "re-

verse fiber" method, they are not only lighter but also more realistic-looking. I first used clear nail polish for the "shaping" process, and still sometimes do, for that matter, but the extensions have a tendency to get a little stiff. General Electric's Silicone Seal, or "super glue" if you wish, has solved the problem of stiffness. The silicone is clear and comes in a tube. If used sparingly, it can be applied to a feather to be reversed and made into an extension without adding a great deal to its weight. When it is dry, usually within one hour or so, the extension feels very much like rubber and is very flexible and durable. The same amount of silicone can be applied on top of the thorax and on the front of the legs on the caddis pupa imitations to prevent the leg fur from flaring out too much.

3-1 G.E. Silicone Seal makes a clear, rubberlike strengthener.

SPRAY ADHESIVE

To prevent splitting and for ease of dressing, the wing quills from which segments are cut and attached to nymph and pupa imitations can be sprayed with an acrylic coating which makes them quite durable without sacrificing the natural flex that exists in most feathers. I use Krylon Crystal Clear #1303, or Flecto Varathane #91-Satin. I have found very little difference between the two, at least for my purposes, and they both dry very quickly. Most paint or hardware stores carry them and a can will last a long time.

FELT-TIP MARKING PENS

The use of waterproof marking pens in fly-tying is nothing new. It is an easy, convenient method of achieving the two-toned effect so often needed when copying insects with a distinct color difference between the top and bottom. The mistake that many have made is to use dime-store markers that are not waterproof. Then the markings fade and wash away after the

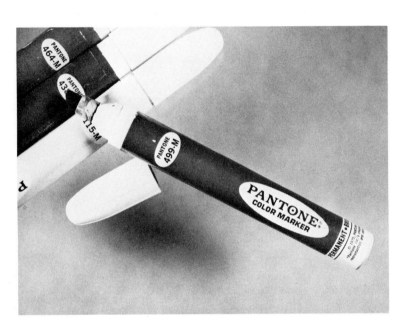

3-2 Pantone felt-tip pens
come in a huge range of colors,
are easy to use, and are waterproof.

For tinting work on artificials, including those in this book, I use the following colors:

Black M	Black
#154M	Brown
#464M	Brown
#499M	Mahogany
#438M	Dark brownish purple
#404M	Gray
#413M	Palest gray (can be used as a neutral color)
#162M	Creamish pink
#176M	Light rosy pink
#136M	Bright yellow
#150M	Bright orange
#165M	Reddish orange
#583M	Light green
#104M	Light olive
#347M	Grass green
#115M	Yellow

Like so many things in fly-tying, an individual's taste in colors is personal, and insects found in different parts of the country may vary in shade and not completely coincide with the colors I have chosen. By all means use your own judgment.

LEAD WIRE

For additional weight on nymphs and other subaquatic artificials, lead wire can

first trip in the water. After experimenting with various brands of pens, I have come to the conclusion that the Pantone Markers are superior for our type of work and come in a full range of colors, and then some. Availability is an important factor when recommending a product, and marking pens are no exception. Pantone pens can be purchased in any reasonably well-stocked art supply store. While in the store, ask the clerk for a color chart for future reference.

be purchased wound on spools or in a coil ready to use. The diameter of the wire should be selected carefully to suit the size of the fly. The most commonly used diameters are from .010 to .035, which is not to say that others are not useful at one time or another, but most dressings in this book do not call for any smaller or larger than those in this range. When dressing the larger stone fly nymphs I often use heavy monofilament to tie onto the sides of a hook shank when an especially wide body is needed.

FLOSS AND WOOL

Although none of my patterns calls for floss or wool to be used as a finishing material, it is often used to wind over an underbody on large nymphs to build it up before applying fur or latex. The floss can be either silk or nylon and comes on spools with single or four-strand lengths. I prefer the four-strand, which is quicker to use when building up a heavy body, and if need be, I cut a single strand from the same spool for smaller flies. A good crewel wool is all you need for under-bodies and comes in many colors from your supplier or department store. Either single-strand or four-strand will do nicely. Choose your colors of floss and wool so they are similar to that of the underbody, or the translucency of fur or latex may give the finished fly a different shade than was intended.

Tails for Nymphs

Tail materials for nymphs are not hard to get; you probably already have most of the feathers in your material stock.

The goose-wing quill fibers for stone flies are taken from the leading edge of the feather (short fibered side on a pointer), where they are usually a little firmer than on the other side of the quill stem. The reason for using white goose quills is to enable the tyer to tint them with the same color marking pen as the rest of the fly.

The two feathers most widely used for tails on nymphs are wood duck flank feather and cock pheasant center tail. Pheasant feathers vary in shade from tan to brown and purplish brown. The fibers are quite strong and are far preferable to anything else for nymphs within their color range. Fibers from wood duck flank feathers are pale olive brown with fine brown markings and imitate well the tails on many of our common nymphs.

To best imitate the fanlike hairy tails on some swimming and burrowing nymphs there is nothing better and more realistic than the tips from mini-ostrich herl, the dun-gray color in particular. They are hard to get from your supplier, but often you can buy a feather duster in a household supply store made from just such feathers, which should give you a lifetime supply.

I can think of only one occasion where peacock herl is used for tails—on the *Isonychia* nymph. Tips from the metallic-green herl turn brown when underwater, and, if I am not mistaken, the entire nymph is often dressed from herl for that reason.

Tails for Dry Flies

Unlike traditional dry flies, which depend heavily on their tails to float in the proper manner, the tails on the flies in this book are of little consequence; at the most, they play a minor role in adding to the attractiveness of the fly. Perhaps in the case of the spinner they aid in stabilizing the fly and keeping the heavier end of the hook from submerging completely. Therefore, the best and stiffest hackle you've set aside for tails should be reserved for spinner imitations, and the less desirable should be used for tails that are set up at an angle so that they rarely come in contact with water. Aside from hackle fibers, it's possible to use wood duck flank feathers and moose or elk mane, materials that formerly would have been sneered at by most, at least for tailing of dry flies.

Feathers for Abdomen Extensions

I mentioned earlier that the materials list includes feathers rarely used in fly dressing. Those for extensions fall into that category. They do so simply because of the characteristics needed in feathers for such work. They must in most cases be body feathers or small spade hackles with a good webby portion that will make the fibers bulky enough when set in glue and compressed into the form of the mayfly abdomen. While I prefer small spade hackles where the fibers in the tip end are usually nice and stiff for imitating tails in the end of the body, I also use the yellowish-tan breast from cock pheasant, wood duck, teal, and mallard flank feathers in their natural colors or dyed to imitate a particular insect. For the smallest realistics where bulk is a major problem, I prefer a small hen neck hackle if the right color is available, or use the simplified extensions of trimmed and lacquered hackle explained in subsequent chapters.

Wings for Dry Flies

Our forefathers would probably turn over in their graves if they found out that anything as simple as deer body hair was being used for winging of dry flies, and yet it beats anything else I've ever tried. The fine-textured hair is best and causes less flare and bulk when fastened on the hook. When tied in, the butt ends are trimmed to form an underbody that, in combination with the fur, makes the flies all but unsinkable. However, care must be taken when selecting the deer hair so the sometimes heavily marked hair tips do not clash with the overall color scheme of the artificial; if necessary, they must even be

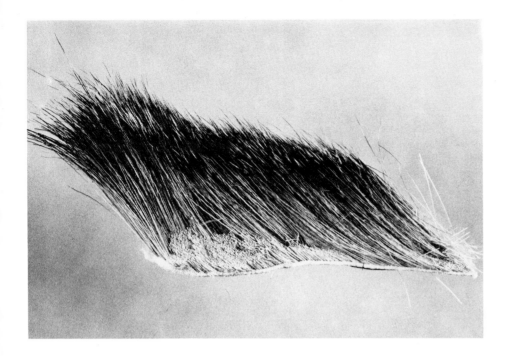

3-3 Deer body hair is an excellent material for dry-fly wings.

3-4 Body feathers can be used for wings on cut-wing patterns or for extensions on mayflies. Left to right: back feather from cock pheasant, metallic neck feather from cock pheasant, yellow breast feather from cock pheasant, flank feather from wood duck.

dyed to resemble the color of the natural insect wings.

There is no doubt that wings are important for added effectiveness of an artificial fishing fly, and those trimmed to shape from thin, delicate body feathers of a blue-dun rooster or hen in different shades very closely resemble the real thing. For the smallest flies I can think of, there is nothing I'd rather use than small neck feathers from a hen. These small feathers are usually wide and firm enough to trim well, and they have a curve in the stem that is almost perfect to produce the proper amount of wing separation when they are set together upright on the hook. There are, of course, many other usable feathers, but most are either not delicate enough or the stems are too heavy and curved. While the aforementioned are ideally suited for flies with wings of a blue-gray or pale-blue-dun color, there are insects for which they are definitely not suitable because the natural insects feature heavily marked wings of an entirely different shade. However, there are other feathers that lend themselves well to this work. Although not as desirable in quality, mallard, teal, and wood duck feathers have markings resembling the naturals, as do the small gray and brown partridge body hackles, all of which can be dyed if necessary. The most natural-looking of them all, however, is a feather I use for the March Brown. It is found on the back of a cock pheasant near the root of the tail. The markings and general color make for a very convincing set of wings.

Wings for Caddis Dry Flies

The traditional method of winging the caddis adult was to use a wing quill segment dressed low-wing in a roof-like manner and then trimmed a bit in the end. It was a fragile arrangement; like other quill wings, it would split rather quickly and ruin the fly's appearance and performance. This has in later years been changed to a better, more durable wing structure of hair. The silhouette of a small bunch of deer body hair or the guard hairs from the very popular mink tail can't be beat. Mink tails are available from your supplier in a variety of colors specifically chosen with caddis dry flies in mind. Fine-textured deer body hair with or without markings is readily available; most fly-tyers have it in their material stock anyway.

Wings for Terrestrials

Wing arrangements on the terrestrial insects of value to the fly-fisherman are relatively simple, consisting in some cases of a combination under and over wing, a dressing method creating a better silhouette. The cricket and hopper imitations are good examples of such wing arrangements. It is best to use natural crow wing quill sections on the cricket, although suppliers may not have it and just give you dyed black mallard, which is acceptable if it is well dyed. The hopper uses a mottled-brown turkey-wing quill section of medium shade. When buying the wing feathers, it is best to get a matched pair even though only a segment from one feather is needed. There are probably other flies you can use the matched feathers for.

Deer body hair is used on both insects, either in its natural color or dyed black. The same black deer hair is used for dressing the black beetle, and when you see a piece of well-dyed material you shouldn't hesitate to grab it, as most dye jobs are poor and the surface will often be crisp and disintegrated.

Feathers for wings on the "Feather Beetle" are from the collar of a cock pheasant. The metallic-colored feathers around the neck—the "ring neck"—are not easy to get from a supplier. If you have a friend who hunts, ask him to bring a bird to you for a "harvest," or perhaps a complete skinning job.

Wing Cases for Nymphs and Caddis Pupae

The latex and fur wing-case arrangements on mayfly and stone fly nymphs are discussed elsewhere in this chapter.

Wing cases for nymphs and pupae are made from quill segments that have been sprayed with Krylon. A good assortment should include turkey, mallard, teal, and two others which are not wing quills but tail feathers—the dark-brown mottled turkey tail for the hellgrammite and the short tail from a cock pheasant for the *Stenonema* nymphs. When a plain shade is called for, it can be taken from a hen wing or dyed mallard. As in many other instances, there are no set rules for the type of feathers used as long as they are similar to those called for in the dressing.

HACKLE

It was the scarcity of good hackle that led me to decide there was a future for flies that require no floating hackle; a couple of turns of "half-good" hackle will at least represent the insect legs and stabilize the fly while it floats in its fur body. This is by no means a new idea, merely an old method that has become popular lately. The reason, I suspect, is the same as mine—there is simply not enough good hackle to go around.

It is always best to buy whole necks rather than loose hackles that might be taken from different birds and are not uniform in color. Even though only one hackle is required for the mayfly duns, the caddis dry flies deserve two of the best "same-colored" hackles you can get.

The following is a listing of the rooster and hen necks, and whole rooster saddles, I most frequently use:

WHITE: These hackles will often have a creamy shine on top; they are better than the pure white, which are generally of poor quality. White hackles are needed for dyeing to particular shades that are so often not obtainable.

CREAM: While the white hackles may have cream in them, it is usually pale; the color you need is somewhere between a white and a very pale ginger.

LIGHT GINGER: A pale-tan shade.

DARK GINGER: A very light brown shade.

NATURAL RED: These hackles have a color that is somewhere between brown and reddish-brown.

COACHMAN BROWN: These hackles from a saddle make good extensions for the *Isonychia* Realistic, etc. The shade is a sort of flat brown to mahogany.

COCH-Y-BONDHU: A dark-brown shade with black edges. I use this particular combination for extensions on the *Leptophlebia* realistics.

FURNACE: These hackles are brown to dark brown, with a black center stripe running down the middle. Sometimes you find hackles on a skin that are shiny ginger-colored with a black stripe. They are very effective for the parachute leg hackle; they produce darkened areas near the wing on top of the thorax, and yet the legs are very light.

BADGER: These are important to me and I use them frequently. Shades in these hackles vary from white to gold edges with a black center stripe. While the white-edged ones have their uses, I prefer the golden badger for the Green Drake and some of the Blue Wing Olives. The rarest variations are those hackles with a bronze-colored edge, and needless to say, they are also very useful for many important dressings of the season.

GRIZZLY: These have black and white bars and come from Plymouth Rock hens and roosters. The ones I prefer, though, are the variants with shades from ginger to golden ginger and brown all mixed in a combination on one hackle. They are, of course, strictly freaks and referred to as "Grizzly Multi-Variants." They are particularly effective for parachute hackle on March Browns and the Gray Foxes. If they are not available, the ordinary grizzly can be dyed any color.

BLUE DUN: Natural blue-dun necks are not only hard to get, but also hard to describe. Over the years I have had necks that ranged from almost completely black to very palest gray. Before you spend your hard-earned dollars on the natural necks,

which, incidentally, are rarely of good quality, look into Eric Leiser's photo-dyed necks. They are nothing less than spectacular in every sense of the word. By photo-dying different shades—for example, a ginger—of natural necks, he is able to come up with a rusty dun, pale-blue dun, and many of the medium-to-dark shades so often used when dressing the Hendricksons, etc.

FUR

Most experienced fly-tyers will agree that fur is the most important material used in the dressing of artificial flies. In fact, I have often stated that if I had to choose one material and discard all the rest, I would never hesitate to keep my fur. The question of which kind of fur is best is, of course, an entirely different story; each individual will usually select the kind that is best suited to the particular flies he is tying. Generally speaking, though, one can divide fur into two categories: the fine-textured mink, beaver, rabbit, opossum, and others which are mostly used for dry flies; and the rougher-textured underfur from such animals as the red and gray fox, woodchuck, and black and brown bear that are primarily used for nymphs and other subaquatic artificials. There are, of course, many others, of which a few will be explained later in the chapter.

The best way of obtaining a great many

different-textured furs is to visit your local furrier and ask if he has any scraps or trimmings he wants to part with. Sometimes you will be doing him a favor by picking it off the floor, and sometimes he will charge you a few bucks, but it's worth it. Also, your material supplier has a long list of fur from which to choose; when looking through the various catalogues it seems as if anything "furry" has a use in fly-tying. However, as you progress in your fly-tying efforts and engage in more advanced work, you will become more selective and more carefully choose the type of fur that has the characteristics you need when dressing a specific insect imitation.

Using the exact fur I prescribe is not nearly as critical for the dry flies in this book as for the nymphs; the dries can be dressed with any of the fine-textured furs mentioned earlier, either in their natural shade or thoroughly dyed.

Fur Dubbing for Dry Flies, Duns, Spinners, and Caddis Flies

While I advocate the use of natural shades, it is just not possible to get the olives, yellows, greens, etc. in natural shades, and they must be dyed. Bleached fur is very good, and many bleached animal furs turn fine creamish or tan shades that are used alone or blended with other colors. Mink fur is the best I can think of, and it is now available in a full range of natural and dyed colors from Fly Fisherman's Bookcase, which handles Eric Leiser's fine products. (See also the list of suppliers at the end of this chapter.)

Fur Dubbing for Nymphs

If you have jumped ahead in this book and looked at the tying instructions and materials lists for the various nymphs, you will have found that there is a considerable difference between my patterns and the traditional dressings of yesterday, both in the material used and in the method of tying. This is not to make things more difficult, but rather to help the fly dresser of today who seeks to achieve more realism in his artificials and who wishes to learn new and practical ways of doing it.

Until recently I was using baby seal's fur for dubbing the abdomen, and I rarely mixed it with anything except an occasional touch of gray beaver to get a dirty shade, or with other colors for the dubbing used when dressing the smaller flies where pure seal would be too coarse. Now that seals are on the Endangered Species List, one cannot depend on anything but the present small supply already on hand, so there is a need for a good substitute. Thanks to modern technology I was able to secure a type of material that apparently has all the characteristics of the real thing. It has an even better sheen, and the texture is such that it can easily be dubbed on your tying thread. But best of

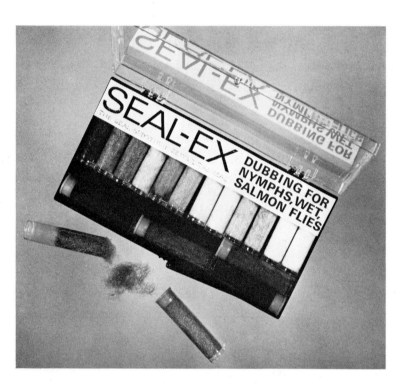

3-5 Seal-Ex dubbing is available in eighteen colors, and in my experience is even better than real seal fur.

Fur for Legs, Thorax, and Wing Case

This is by far the most important and most difficult type of fur to select, and I can't emphasize strongly enough that you take your time in selecting and practicing the method of dubbing the legs, thorax, and wing case in one application. For this work the fur must be taken off the skin unblended, because the secret to success lies in using the guard hairs and underfur as it is cut from the skin, with the natural direction of both being undisturbed.

The two types that I like best for all my nymphs are, first, the belly, neck, leg, and mask of an Australian opossum; and second, the well-marked guard hair and fur from the back of a brown rabbit. If you are lucky enough to obtain a complete skin of an Australian opossum, you have covered your needs for mayfly nymphs. The brown rabbit with its longer back fur and well-marked guard hairs is primarily used for legs and thorax on caddis pupae and larger stone fly nymphs, but there is no set rule as long as either fur will produce the desired result. Choosing the proper length of fur is the important thing, and while brown rabbit is not hard to get (some surplus stores around the country sell whole skins for a couple of dollars), the opossum may have to be purchased in small pieces from which you can select what you need. The alternatives are mink and hare's mask, and I am sure there are others just as useful.

all, the translucency of this high-quality substitute is magnificent. When dubbed on the abdomen portion of a nymph it can be trimmed flat, and you can pick it out to imitate the gills that are present on most nymphs. It is called Seal-Ex and is now available from your supplier in sets of eighteen different colors for mixing.

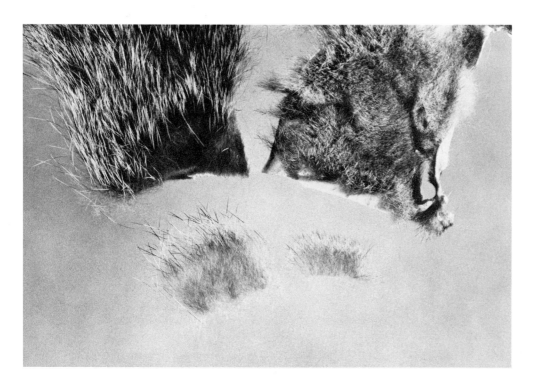

3-6 On left, well-marked back
fur from rabbit. On right, short
fur and guard hairs from face
and neck of Australian
opossum.

PREPARING LEG, THORAX, AND WING-CASE FUR

In most cases the fur need not be dyed, because the natural gray, brown, tan, and creamish colors are already found on the skin. However, brown rabbit skins should always be dyed in the color indicated in the pattern for the various nymphs and pupae, because the two-toned guard hairs have too much contrast. A simple dye bath can be prepared by heating two cups of water in a saucepan and adding two teaspoons of Rit Dye (from your dime store) and one tablespoon of white vinegar. The water need not come to a boil,

3-7 Fur is easy to dye in Rit, a fabric dye that is available almost anywhere.

but the dye powder must be completely dissolved. When the dye bath has cooled enough for you to stick a finger in it without getting burned, it is ready. Cut the fur in 2-inch-wide strips about 4 or 5 inches long and wash it thoroughly in a mild soapy solution before inserting it into the dye bath. The length of time it should be kept in the bath depends on the color

being dyed and must be determined by experimentation. Remember, the color is always darker when the material is wet. If the result is not right the first time, it is usually too light, so add some more dye and give it another turn until you are satisfied.

Rinse the fur under cold running water as soon as it comes out of the bath, hold-

3-8 Don't blot the dyed and rinsed fur; hang it up to drip-dry so that the hairs will not be disarranged.

3-9 Blended fur can be kept in small labeled containers, so that you will always have the right shade handy for the patterns you tie the most.

ing it so that the stream runs in the natural direction of the fur and guard hair and brings them back to order. Once this is done I clamp a clothespin on the edge of the skin and hang it up to dry near the furnace or in the sunlight, letting the water run off rather than pressing it between newspaper, which would disarrange the fur again.

CUTTING THE FUR LAYER

I mentioned earlier that the length of the fur is important, and I would like to repeat this. Legs on the nymphs are usually sized to be half a body length (with perhaps the exception of the large *Hexagenia* and *Ephemera,* which are about one-third a body length). A good guideline to remember about the length is to make them as long as two hook gaps. Personally, I prefer the legs to be too short rather than too long, but that is strictly an individual preference. Fig. 3-6 illustrates two different types of fur. One is a piece of back fur from a brown rabbit and the other a piece of opossum. Both are used for the thorax/leg construction, and the fur layer which has been cut from the edge of the skin clearly illustrates the difference in fiber length. The rule to follow when selecting the fur is quite simple—the smaller the fly the softer the fur. Opossum is generally used for flies from Size 12 and down, while rabbit is used for anything larger than that. The rabbit back fur may feel soft to you, but when cut from the skin and trimmed to length, the guard hairs are actually very stiff. Of course, all fur and guard hair is not of the same length all over an animal and it is always a good practice to keep pieces of skin from different parts of the pelt handy.

When a thin fur layer has been cut from the edge of a piece of skin it will nearly always have to be trimmed to length. This is done by holding the fur by the tips and trimming the butt portion.

LATEX

Until Raleigh Boaze, Jr., discovered the use of latex as the ultimate answer to the fly-tyer's need for a super body material, I thought that everything that could possibly be wound, spun, or glued on a hook had been tried. Raleigh has started a brand-new chapter in American fly-tying. The full impact of his discovery has not yet been felt, and I predict that the future will bring many new artificials into popularity, all using latex in one form or another.

The material is available from your supplier in small 5 × 5-inch sheets that can be cut in strips of any width. Do not be misled into thinking that very thin latex can be used. The thickness best suited for flies is designated by the manufacturer as Heavy, .0112 to .0115. To cut it one can use a paper cutter (see Fig. 3-10) or simply a sharp razor blade or X-Acto knife. Either way I find it best to sandwich the latex between two pieces of cardboard or it is difficult to control. The width of the strips needed for a particular nymph is indicated in its pattern. Latex can be dyed as you would dye fur and feathers, and it is easily tinted with waterproof marking pens.

SUPPLIERS OF FLY-TYING MATERIALS

Harry and Elsie Darbee
Livingston Manor, New York 12758

Fireside Angler
Box 823
Melville, New York 11746

3-10 A paper cutter does a neat job of cutting latex strips if the latex sheet is sandwiched between cardboard.

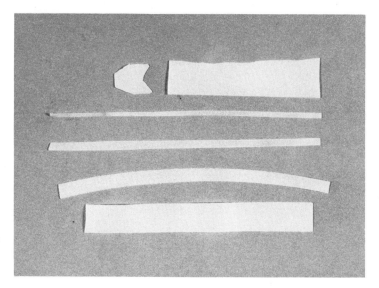

3-11 Latex ready for use. The arrow-shaped piece is for a stone fly wing case.

Materials
37

Fly Fisherman's Bookcase Tackle Service
Route 9A
Croton-on-Hudson, New York 10520

E. Hille
815 Railway Street
Williamsport, Pennsylvania 17701

Jack's Tackle
301 Bridge Street
Phoenixville, Pennsylvania 19460

Bud Lilly's Fly Shop
West Yellowstone, Montana 59758

E. Veniard, Ltd.
138 Northwood Road
Thornton Heath, Surrey, England

4
Mayfly Nymphs

TYPES OF NATURAL MAYFLY NYMPHS

The nymphal forms of our mayflies are very important to the angler who expects to achieve some degree of success, and they constitute a considerable portion of a fish's diet. They are found in most Eastern and Western streams capable of generating sufficient oxygen for them to live. Unlike adult mayflies, which are almost identical in appearance in all species, the nymphs are different. They can be divided into four groups of particular interest to the angler, each with some structural characteristics of its own, and each with an individual choice of habitat.

Conventional nymph patterns used in the past almost without exception used only color and size as their principal identification features, and this may have limited their effectiveness as representa-

tives for specific nymphs. The discovery of new materials and techniques and the high development of fly-tying skill in America have now made it possible to treat each nymphal form individually, with special attention to the main features that characterize the particular insect it was made to imitate.

Clinging Species

The nymphs of this group are very flat and rather broad anteriorly, with flat, robust-looking legs. They can be found clinging to the underside of rocks and other objects where they are well hidden from predators. They inhabit fast water with plenty of oxygen, but before hatching they move to shallow areas where they can easily be collected if specimens are needed

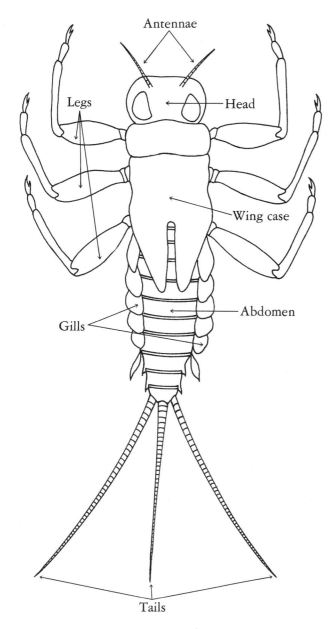

Anatomy of mayfly nymph

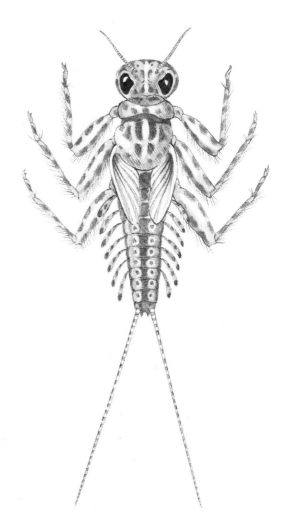

Mayfly nymph, clinger

as models. The ones best known are those of the *Stenonema* and *Iron* genera.

Burrowing Species

This type of nymph is the most unusual and interesting one. Like a mole, it plows its way through the muddy bottom and debris. The structure of the burrowing nymph makes it easy to recognize. It is rather long, slender, and oval in cross section, with flattened legs and a large tusk-like projection on either side of the abdomen; on artificial flies these projections are referred to as gills. The *Ephemera* and

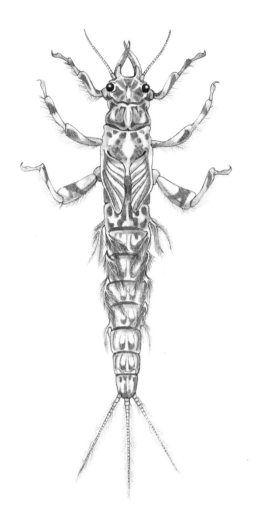

Mayfly nymph, burrower

the large *Hexagenia* nymphs belong to the burrowing group.

Sprawling Species

Nymphs belonging to the sprawling group move around slowly in all types of water, where they inhabit vegetation, gravel, and debris. The legs are thin and rather feeble in comparison with the clingers, and their bodies are round or oval in cross section, depending on the species. Specimens can be collected in a seine by shaking vegetation or moving debris on the stream bottom. Genera include *Ephemerella*, *Leptophlebia*, and *Caenis*.

Climber Species

These are free-ranging nymphs found in fast water where they dart, run, or swim around in the vegetation like minnows. They are very slender and streamlined with feeble legs like the sprawlers. The body is oval and the tails are usually heavily fringed. They can be collected in the same manner as the sprawlers.

The group to which a particular nymph belongs will be indicated with each dressing pattern in this chapter. In most cases the structural differences between one nymph and another depend mostly on the amount of material used and how it is trimmed or picked out before or after being applied on the hook. As an example, if a nymph is very flat with long gills, the fur for the abdomen should be teased up before it is wound on the hook, and the body should be trimmed more on the top and bottom than one with an oval shape. If a nymph has medium to short gills, the fur need not be teased and the

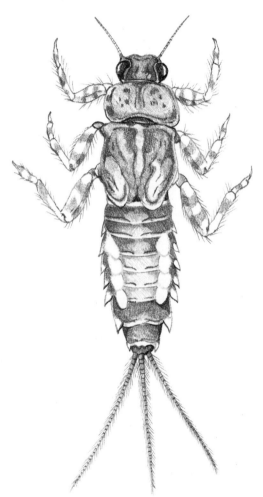

Mayfly nymph, sprawler

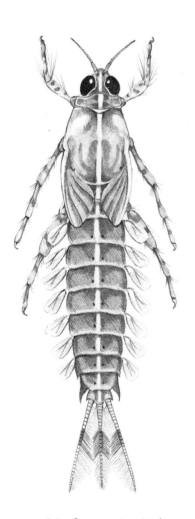

Mayfly nymph, climber

trimming will usually bring out sufficient fibers to imitate gills. What really is achieved with this method of dressing is a translucency and silhouette not possible with any other method that I know of.

DRESSING THE MAYFLY NYMPH, STEP BY STEP

I have chosen the *Stenonema* nymph as a model for the dressing instructions because of its large size and claim to fame as a good fish-getter. The nymphs belong to a group of several clingers of importance to the angler. Their flattish appearance can be well imitated by using the loop method to spin the dubbing. There are three related species of the *Stenonema* genus that are almost identical and with which the angler should be familiar: *S. vicarium* (March Brown), the largest of the three; *S. fuscum* (Gray Fox), the middle-sized representative; and *S. canadense* (Light Cahill), the smallest of the group. Since they are all so well known, none should go unmentioned, but for all practical purposes, the only difference between the three, at least as far as angling is concerned, is the size.

THE STENONEMA NYMPH

COMMON NAMES	March Brown, Gray Fox Light Cahill
GENUS	*Stenonema*
SPECIES	*vicarium, fuscum, canadense*

AVAILABILITY These nymphs are quite common in Eastern and Midwestern streams capable of generating sufficient oxygen. When they are ready to hatch (hatching usually starts in late May and lasts through mid-June, depending on temperature and locale), the nymphs migrate to shallow areas and during such times are often deadly and irresistible to the fish.

Very often the adults have some difficulty in escaping the nymphal skin, or for other reasons are unable to leave the water surface immediately and find themselves floating and struggling for a long time, a circumstance which permits the trout to feed on them in a leisurely manner without expending too much energy. For this reason an emerger-type artificial is often needed to get the full benefit of a hatch. The best known is the Hare's Ear, for which the dressing is listed in the section with additional nymph dressings. The other is the nymph dressing covered in the tying instructions, with one notable difference. The wingcase fur is left long, untrimmed, and unlacquered, thus giving the appearance of a partly emerged dun, or a struggling one unable to take off. The artificial should not be weighted, but instead must be given some dry-fly flotant, usually a silicone type like Gehrke's Gink, which can be smeared lightly on the underside.

BODY LENGTH	9 to 16mm
HOOK	Mustad #38941, Size 10 to 12 and Mustad #3906B, Size 12 to 16
THREAD	Brown, prewaxed 6/0
TAILS	Three brown fibers from cock pheasant center tail, one hook length long

4-1 Dressing the *Stenonema* nymph, Step 1.

ABDOMEN	Pale-amber Seal-Ex dubbing tinted brown on top
GILLS	Medium, roughed-up dubbing
THORAX AND LEGS	Bleached opossum fur with guard hairs, or rabbit dyed tannish-amber; material applied fairly heavy
WING CASE	Trimmed thorax fur lacquered, or segment from short pheasant tail, underside up, or latex dyed dark brown and trimmed
HEAD	Brown tying thread
DUBBING FORMULA	1 part reddish-brown, 2 parts yellow, and 3 parts cream, mixed

TINTING   Since this nymph is lighter underneath than it is on top, the back is tinted lightly with brown Pantone #154. This is not a solid tint and the amber should show on the back for the best effect. If a *fur* wing case is used, it should be tinted with the same color brown as the back of the abdomen. When dyed brown latex is used, the tip of the trimmed wing case is tinted lightly with a gray

4-2 Step 2.

4-3 Step 3.

Pantone Marker #404M to produce a blackish effect like the wing-case tips of the natural.

1. Tie in the tail fibers securely on the shank above a point midway between the hook point and the barb. I have never found that it makes any difference whether the fibers are splayed as the natural at rest or not. If additional weight is needed, it should be applied now. This can best be done by tying in a lead strip on one side of the hook shank and covering it with tying thread so that the flatness of the body can be maintained. Now form

a spinning loop where the tails are tied in and insert a generous amount of dubbing.

2. Spin a ropelike dubbing that is fairly tight, well tapered, and heavy.

3. Rough up the dubbing with your X-Acto saw. Do this with short, quick movements all the way around and for the full length of the dubbing. Care should be taken to only rough up the dubbing, not rip off the fibers as they will aid in achieving the flatness in the body and also represent the medium-sized gills on the sides of the abdomen.

4-4 Step 4.

4-5 Step 5.

4. Apply some clear cement on the hook shank and wind the dubbing on the shank with close turns, stroking back the loosened fibers in the process and thus creating a fuzzy-looking body portion. Tie off about one-third hook length from the eye and make a couple of half-hitches.

5. Trim the body on top and bottom with your scissors. Not only cut the fuzzy dubbing, but also dig in a little in the solid stuff without cutting the dubbing thread. This is best done by holding the scissors horizontal and lengthwise with the body, then making short, quick clipping motions with the points of the scissors. Trim it the full body length. Trim the sides lightly to remove long, stray fibers, but leave the side dubbing long enough to represent the

4-6 Step 6.

4-7 Step 7.

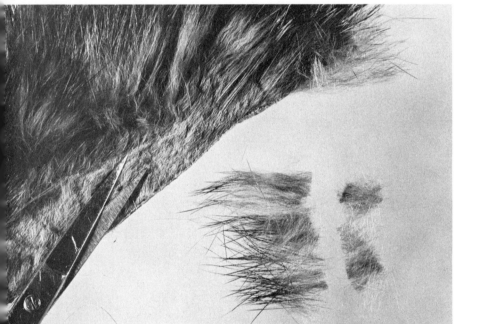

gills. To be sure of a firm body, compress it slightly by pushing from the front to the rear. The abdomen occupies slightly more than half a hook shank.

6. The finished abdomen portion. Note that the body for this particular nymph is rather broad anteriorly, like most clingers, and as all the bodies for this type of nymph, it is segmented and highly translucent. Now form a spinning loop directly in front of the abdomen.

7. Cut a small bunch of fur and guard hairs for the thorax and legs. The whole bunch should be as long as half a body length. Do not disturb the natural direction of the fibers as they are to be used unmixed as they come off of the skin.

Mayfly
Nymphs
47

4-8 Step 8.

4-9a Step 9.

8. Insert the fur into the loop. Note the proportional placement. It is well spread out, and by using the loop thread as a guideline, you will see that the fur bunch is much longer on one side of the loop than on the other. The longer side has the fur and guard hairs that will become the legs, and the short side becomes the thorax and wing case (if a fur wing case is desired).

4-9b Step 9.

4-10 Step 10.

9. Spin a fur chenille by using your heavy pliers as a weight, then hold it up above the hook and moisten it a little before stroking all the fur and guard hairs back so it appears to be coming out from one side of the loop only.

10. Apply a little clear cement on the hook shank, then wind the fur on the thorax portion in front of the abdomen. Tie off in front, cut the surplus, and form a small head.

Mayfly Nymphs 49

4-11a Step 11.

4-11b Step 11.

11. Trim the fur and guard hair on top of the thorax, leaving it long enough to form an average-size wing case. Do not trim away the sides and bottom, as this material represents the legs. Brush or comb the fur a little with your X-Acto saw so that the fibers are parallel with the body, then brush on a coat of clear nail

4-12a Step 12.

4-12b Step 12.

polish. Press it flat a little with your fingers and trim the rear corners.

12. When it is dry, tint the wing case and top of the abdomen with a brown Pantone Marker #154 and the nymph is finished. If you wish, you can trim along the center under the thorax, leaving enough on each side to represent the legs.

Mayfly Nymphs 51

4-13 Adding a quill wing case to an all-fur nymph.

Other Wing-Case Forms

In line with tradition, artificial nymphs are usually dressed with a wing case consisting of a quill section of the proper color tied in in front of the abdomen and folded forward over the thorax and tied down in front. This can also be done on the all-fur nymphs in the following manner:

When the abdomen is finished and before the spinning loop for the leg and thorax fur is made, tie in a quill section of the material specified for the wing case in the pattern. The width of the section should be slightly more than that of the body, and the first tie-in windings must hold the quill section tightly against the front of the abdomen. Cut the surplus short of the eye and wind some thread over the ends to bind them down on the shank. Take the thread to the extreme front of the abdomen and form a spinning loop. At this point the fly should look like Fig. 4-13. Proceed in the same manner as explained in Steps 7, 8, 9, and 10.

4-14 Finished *Stenonema* nymph imitation with wing case.

4-15 Making a latex wing case, Step 1.

Then, divide the fur on top down the middle and press it down to each side of the thorax. Now fold the quill section forward over the thorax and tie off in front. Cut the surplus quill before winding the head and applying some clear cement. The finished *Stenonema* with wing case is shown in Fig. 4-14.

The Latex Wing Case

While I prefer fur and quill-section wing cases on my nymphs, there are some who might find it simpler just to trim all the fur on top of the thorax and tie in a small trimmed section of latex for a wing case. This can be done in the following manner:

1. Trim a 1-inch-long strip of latex as seen in Fig. 4-15. While only a small portion of the length is used, it must be that long so that you can hold it while it is being tied in. The width is a little more than a body width of the nymph being dressed.

2. Lay the strip on top and tie it on in front. The latex must be held tightly when being secured or it will not stay on top. Now cut the surplus in front and leave the end exposed to imitate the head, or trim clean and wind the tying thread over it. The length of the wing case is usually a little shorter than half a body length; any deviation from this measurement will be indicated in the individual patterns.

3. When the latex wing case is first tied in it is possible that it will not lie down absolutely flat. In fact, at times it sits quite high. If this is the case, tint it with a Pantone of the same color as the latex and it automatically falls into place. When the Pantone dries the latex may rise up a little, in which case a little cement can be applied on top of the thorax and underside of the wing case.

SELECTED NYMPH AND IMPORTANT EMERGER AND WET-FLY DRESSINGS

Important note: Also, although I find Seal-Ex to be the best material for nymph bodies, any of the coarser furs like the foxes or the bear and woodchuck may be used if you wish, but they somehow lack the translucency of Seal-Ex. All the nymphs included below, with one exception, can be dressed with either of three wing-case forms:

1. Trimmed, lacquered, and tinted thorax fur

2. Trimmed and tinted latex

3. Wing quill section of the color indicated for the wing case

The *Ephoron* nymph is the exception; the only material used for the case is deer hair. The thorax and leg fur method of dressing may seem awkward in the beginning (see Chapter 3 for fur types), but you will soon get the hang of it, and the amount of time spent learning pays dividends on the stream in the form of *fish*.

The most frustrating experience when fishing a nymph is inability to control the sink rate. I suggest that the nymph be dressed both weighted and unweighted in anticipation of fishing different types of water. The weight, in the form of thin lead wire, may be tied on the sides of the shank for the flat clinger-type nymphs, or simply wound like thread around the hook shank. I rarely use anything heavier than .010 lead wire, which is thin enough not to ruin the appearance of the nymph.

ADOPTIVA NYMPH (CRAWLER)

COMMON NAMES	Blue Quill, Blue Dun, Little Blue Mayfly
GENUS	*Paraleptophlebia*
SPECIES	*adoptiva*

AVAILABILITY   Anglers in the East and Midwest who have enough courage to travel to their favorite stream in the sometime chilly weather of mid-April will probably find the Little Blue Quill on the water, and it usually remains there through May. The little *adoptiva* nymph is very effective shortly after noon, before hatching, when fished at almost any depth; a greased one may be fished successfully right in the surface film.

BODY LENGTH	6 to 8mm
HOOK	Mustad #3906B, Size 16 to 18
THREAD	Brown, prewaxed 6/0
TAILS	Three wood duck fibers, one-half body length
ABDOMEN	Yellow-brown Seal-Ex dubbing
GILLS	Picked out long
THORAX AND LEGS	Medium-brown guard hairs with fur
WING CASE	Dark grayish-brown
HEAD	Brown tying thread
DUBBING FORMULA	3 parts medium brown, 1½ parts yellow
TINTING	Fur or latex wing case tinted dark gray with Pantone #404M

BAETIS NYMPH (SWIMMER)

COMMON NAME	Blue-Wing Olive
GENUS	*Baetis*
SPECIES	Various

AVAILABILITY   *Baetis* are among the most important insects for the trout angler and are present and active on streams throughout the country from April through September. *Baetis vagans,* a Size 16 to 18 medium olive-brown nymph, is particularly useful for those who fish the famous limestone streams of Pennsylvania.

BODY LENGTH	5 to 10mm
HOOK	Mustad #94840, Size 20 Mustad #3906B, Size 16 to 18
THREAD	Olive, prewaxed 6/0
TAILS	Three wood duck fibers, half a body length
ABDOMEN	Seal-Ex or fur: #1. Dark brown #2. Medium olive-brown #3. Dark olive #4. Medium brown
GILLS	Fibers appearing on sides after trimming abdomen are sufficient
THORAX AND LEGS	Grayish-brown guard hairs with fur; on the smallest nymphs a sparse amount of fur is applied and the legs picked out
WING CASE	Dark grayish brown
HEAD	Olive tying thread
DUBBING FORMULA	Dubbing #2: 1 part medium brown and 1 part medium olive

TINTING   Fur on latex wing case tinted with gray Pantone #404M

BLUE-WING OLIVE NYMPH (SPRAWLER)

COMMON NAMES	Blue-Wing Olive, Small Dun Variant, Little Olive Cutwing
GENUS	*Ephemerella*
SPECIES	*attenuata*

AVAILABILITY   This is another of the many super flies in the East, and although the species *E. attenuata* is particularly active prior to hatching, usually in late May and continuing through the better part of June, it lends itself well as a representative for other similar flies found throughout the country and can be dressed in any size. *E. attenuata* is one species that hatches under water like *Epeorus pleuralis* (Quill Gordon), and a wet fly, for which I also give the dressing, often works better than the nymph.

BODY LENGTH	7 to 9mm
HOOK	Mustad #3906B, Size 14 to 16
THREAD	Black, prewaxed 6/0
TAILS	Three wood duck flank feather fibers, two-thirds body length
ABDOMEN	Dark-brownish-olive Seal-Ex dubbing
GILLS	Picked out lightly
THORAX AND LEGS	Medium-olive-brown guard hairs with fur
WING CASE	Black
HEAD	Black tying thread

DUBBING FORMULA	2 parts medium brown, 2 parts light olive, and 1 part black
TINTING	Fur wing case tinted dark

brown with Pantone #154; latex wing case first tinted with brown Pantone #154, then touched up with a little gray Pantone #404M

BLUE-WING OLIVE WET FLY

HOOK	Mustad #3906B, Size 14 to 16
THREAD	Olive, prewaxed 6/0
TAILS	Light-blue-dun hackle fibers
BODY	Yellowish-olive fur dubbing
HACKLE	Medium-blue-dun hen hackle, soft
WINGS	Blue-gray duck-wing quill sections, tied downwing
HEAD	Olive tying thread
DUBBING FORMULA	1 part yellow and 1 part olive fur

CAENIS NYMPH (SPRAWLER)

COMMON NAMES	Angler's Curse, Tiny White-Winged Dun
GENUS	*Tricorythodes*
SPECIES	Various

AVAILABILITY Found throughout the country. Active period from June through September, depending on locale.

BODY LENGTH	4 to 5mm
HOOK	Mustad #3906, Size 18
THREAD	Olive, prewaxed 6/0

TAILS	Three brown fibers from cock pheasant center tail, half a body length
ABDOMEN	Grayish-brown fur dubbing
THORAX AND LEGS	Dark-grayish-brown fur with short guard hairs
WING CASE	Trimmed thorax fur, lacquered and tinted
HEAD	Olive tying thread
DUBBING FORMULA	2 parts medium-brown fur and 1 part medium-gray fur
TINTING	Fur wing case tinted lightly

with gray Pantone #404M

EPEORUS NYMPH (CLINGER)

COMMON NAMES	Gordon Quill, Quill Gordon, Iron Dun
GENUS	*Epeorus*
SPECIES	*pleuralis, fraudator*

AVAILABILITY For many years this fly has been among the best-known in America, and still is for that matter. It is the one fly the angler thinks of at the outset of each new season. Nymphs are active just before a hatch; hatching usually occurs from mid-April through mid-May and starts shortly after noon. Since the fly hatches underwater, it is more effective to use a Quill Gordon wet fly during a hatch, and so I have included the wet-fly dressing below. However, I also use an emerger type of artificial, which is the *Epeorus* nymph with the wing-case fur left long and untrimmed (see Fig. 4-18). This version should be treated to float with a silicone such as Gehrke's Gink and fished in the surface film. Unlike the nymph-type artificial, the emerger

4-18 A *Stenonema* imitation of the emerger type, with the wing-case fur left long and unlacquered on top to represent the wings of the emerging insect.

is unweighted, thus enabling you to fish it right in the surface film.

BODY LENGTH	11 to 15mm
HOOK	Mustad #38941 3X Long, Size 12 to 14 Mustad #3906B, Size 8 to 10
THREAD	Olive, prewaxed 6/0
TAILS	Two brown fibers from cock pheasant tail, one body length
ABDOMEN	Medium-brown Seal-Ex dubbing with a touch of olive
GILLS	Picked out, heavy
THORAX AND LEGS	Medium-brown guard hairs with fur
WING CASE	Medium brown
HEAD	Olive tying thread
DUBBING FORMULA	10 parts medium brown and 1 part medium olive
TINTING	Fur and latex wing case should be tinted with brown Pantone #154M; latex wingtips are touched lightly with gray Pantone #404M

QUILL GORDON WET FLY

HOOK	Mustad #3906B, Size 12 to 14
THREAD	Black, prewaxed 6/0

TAILS	Rusty-blue-dun hackle fibers
BODY	Stripped peacock quill
HACKLE	Rusty-blue-dun hen hackle, soft
WINGS	Wood duck flank feather, tied downwing
HEAD	Black tying thread

EPHEMERA NYMPH
(BURROWER)

COMMON NAMES	Green Drake, Multi-Variant
GENUS	*Ephemera*
SPECIES	*guttulata*

AVAILABILITY This large, beautiful mayfly has undoubtedly stirred up enough action and excitement to deserve a whole chapter of its own. The nymph pattern is a good representative for several flies of the same genus when dressed in different sizes. Although it has often been said that the nymph of a Green Drake is not effective, I have had extremely good luck with a heavily weighted nymph Size 4 3X Long. Cast it upstream, let it sink deep and come down drag-free until it is almost in front of you, then quickly raise it to the surface. That is when the trout hits it.

BODY LENGTH	15 to 28mm
HOOK	Mustad #38941 3X Long, Size 4 to 10
THREAD	Brown, prewaxed 6/0
TAILS	Three light-tannish-gray mini-ostrich herl tips, one-third body length
ABDOMEN	Light-amber Seal-Ex dubbing with brown back markings
GILLS	Abdomen fur teased up before it is wound; pick out gills further after body is trimmed for tusklike heavy gills; may be tinted gray
THORAX AND LEGS	Creamish-amber guard hairs with fur
WING CASE	Medium brown
HEAD	Brown tying thread
DUBBING FORMULA	3 parts cream, 2 parts yellow, and 1 part reddish-brown

TINTING Fur or latex wing case is tinted brown with Pantone #154M; the tips on the latex case are touched lightly with gray Pantone #404M; back markings are made with Pantone #154M; gills tinted with gray Pantone #404M

EPHEMERELLA NYMPH
(CRAWLER)

COMMON NAMES	Hendrickson, Red Quill, Beaverkill
GENUS	*Ephemerella*
SPECIES	*subvaria, invaria, rotunda*

AVAILABILITY This is one of the best-known members of the American fly hatches, at least in the East and Midwest, with some related species found in Western waters. The nymphs are most active and vulnerable to trout from the end of April through the beginning of June before hatching. I have made it one of my standard patterns for nymph fishing all year, both weighted and unweighted.

BODY LENGTH	9 to 12mm
HOOK	Mustad #3906B, Size 10 to 12
THREAD	Brown, prewaxed 6/0
TAILS	Three light-brown fibers from cock pheasant center tail, one-half body length
ABDOMEN	Reddish-amber Seal-Ex dubbing, touch-tinted on the back
GILLS	Picked out, medium
THORAX AND LEGS	Well-marked brown guard hairs with fur
WING CASE	Dark brown
HEAD	Brown tying thread
DUBBING FORMULA	2 parts cream, 1 part reddish brown, and 1 part yellow

TINTING   Fur or latex wing case is tinted dark brown with Pantone #154M; in addition, the tips on the trimmed latex case are touched lightly with gray Pantone #404M; the back of the abdomen is dabbed lightly with brown Pantone #154M, leaving the center one-third an untouched reddish-amber color; if you wish, the back can be left as is, without tint

EPHORON NYMPH
(BURROWER)

COMMON NAMES	White Fly, White Miller
GENUS	*Ephoron*
SPECIES	Representative

AVAILABILITY   These white flies are found in some Eastern and Midwestern streams, and I have experienced blizzardlike hatches at twilight during the last two weeks of July on the Potomac River in western Maryland and in late August and September on the Yellow Breeches in Pennsylvania. The nymphs are active from late afternoon before a hatch, and they are fished as an emerger in most cases.

BODY LENGTH	11 to 13mm
HOOK	Mustad #38941 3X Long, Size 12 to 14
THREAD	Gray, prewaxed 6/0
TAILS	Three grayish-white wing quill fibers, one-third body length
ABDOMEN	Dirty-white Seal-Ex and fur dubbing
GILLS	Picked out, heavy
THORAX AND LEGS	Grayish-white fur with guard hairs
WING CASE	Medium-gray deer body hair over thorax, lacquered
HEAD	Gray tying thread
DUBBING FORMULA	White Seal-Ex dubbing with gray fur added to produce a dirty-white color

TINTING   If natural deer body hair is used for the wing case, it should be tinted medium gray with Pantone #404M

Note: A small piece of orange silk floss is often added in front of the thorax as a beard before the head is wound. It should not be more than $1/16$ inch long. According to anglers on the Yellow Breeches, it makes the nymph more effective. The

4-19 A *Hexagenia* imitation. This is typical of the large burrowing nymphs. Note the heavily picked-out dubbing representing the tusklike gills.

reason for having a deer-hair wing is to fish the nymph in the surface film with the front in the film and the abdomen riding downward at an angle. The front is often dressed with silicone flotant to achieve this.

HEXAGENIA NYMPH (BURROWER)

COMMON
NAMES   Michigan Caddis, Fish Fly

GENUS   *Hexagenia*

SPECIES   Various

AVAILABILITY   While flies of the *Hexagenia* genus are found in both Eastern and Midwestern waters, they are best known for their appearance on Michigan streams from mid-June through the better part of August, de-

pending on the area being fished. I use weighted versions of the *Hexagenia* nymph all year round, and the fish are always looking for a good-size meal, even early in the season.

BODY LENGTH   16 to 30mm

HOOK   Mustad #38941 3X Long, Size 4

THREAD   Brown, prewaxed 6/0

TAILS   Three light-tannish-gray mini-ostrich herl tips, one-third body length

ABDOMEN   Amber Seal-Ex dubbing mixed with gray fur; purple-brown back markings at each abdomen segment

GILLS   Abdomen fur teased up before being wound; after trimming top and bottom, pick out the gills further for

Mayfly
Nymphs
61

tusklike heavy gills; may be tinted

THORAX AND LEGS	Tan guard hairs with fur
WING CASE	Purplish-brown, one-third body length
HEAD	Brown tying thread
DUBBING FORMULA	1 part reddish brown, 2 parts yellow, 3 parts cream with medium-gray fur added to get a dirty or grayish amber

TINTING   Fur or latex wing case tinted purplish brown with Pantone #438M; back markings and light tinting of the gills are done with the same color marker

ISONYCHIA NYMPH (CLIMBER)

COMMON NAMES	Dun Variant, White Gloved Howdy, Leadwing Coachman
GENUS	*Isonychia*
SPECIES	*bicolor, sadleri*

AVAILABILITY   Evening hatches of the slim, fast-swimming *Isonychia* nymphs take place on Eastern and Midwestern streams from late May through August. Aside from the stone flies, this is the only nymph that I know of that crawls onto stones and debris out of the water to hatch. The exoskeletons are found along the rocky streamside and can be used for models, although such specimens are very fragile and should be handled with care. The best thing to do is to take a closeup photograph for your file. I usually weight these nymphs and find that they work better when applying a swim-

ming action. As is the case with several other nymphs included in my list of important dressings, there is a related wet-fly pattern worthy of note. Who can forget the Leadwing Coachman with the sparkling peacock herl and slate-gray wings for an evening of good fishing? I have included the dressing below the nymph pattern for those who feel as I do that it's a "darn good fly."

BODY LENGTH	16 to 20mm
HOOK	Mustad #38941 3X Long, Size 8 to 10
THREAD	Brown, prewaxed 6/0
TAILS	Three peacock herl tips, one-third body length
ABDOMEN	Dark-purple-brown Seal-Ex dubbing with thin white medium stripe of goose-quill fiber or light moose-mane fiber tied down over abdomen and wing case (stripe optional)
GILLS	Picked out, medium long
THORAX AND LEGS	Short well-marked grayish guard hairs and fur from hare's or opossum's mask
WING CASE	Dark grayish brown (wing case is rather pronounced and only one-third body length)
HEAD	Brown tying thread
DUBBING FORMULA	4 parts medium brown, 2 parts black, 1 part magenta, and 1 part reddish brown

TINTING   Fur or latex wing case is tinted with dark-brown Pantone #154M; in addition, the latex is also given a light touch of

4-20 An *Isonychia* imitation, top and side views. Note the white center stripe and latex wing case. The long slender form is typical of the climbing group.

gray Pantone #404M to produce the dark-grayish-brown shade

Note: If you wish to dress the nymph with the white medium stripe on top, it is done in the following manner. When the tails have been tied in, tie in a 6-inch length of purple-colored tying thread, together with a white fiber from a goose wing quill or a light moose-mane fiber. The two materials should sit on top of the shank. Proceed to finish the abdomen por-

tion, then lay the fiber over the top in the middle and use the purple thread to secure it. Tie it off in front of the abdomen. Do not cut the surplus fiber. When the thorax, leg portion, and wing case are finished, including tinting, the remainder is laid forward over the wing case and tied down in front before the head is wound, thus making the white stripe run the full length of the nymph. This is done only on the *bicolor* species; on *sadleri* the stripe is of little consequence.

LEADWING COACHMAN
WET FLY

HOOK	Mustad #3906B, Size 8 to 10
THREAD	Black, prewaxed 6/0
TAIL	None; instead, a small flat gold tinsel tag
BODY	Peacock herl, fairly thick
HACKLE	Reddish-brown hen hackle
WINGS	Lead-colored starling wing quill sections
HEAD	Black tying thread

LEPTOPHLEBIA NYMPH
(SPRAWLER)

COMMON NAMES	Black Quill, Whirling Dun, Cutwing Leptophlebia
GENUS	*Leptophlebia*
SPECIES	*cupida*

AVAILABILITY This dark-brown nymph is active all through the day from late April through early June. Eastern anglers have used these dark nymphs for many years as an "all-purpose" nymph when dark flies abound, but since there are several related species found in Western waters, it is certainly not restricted to Eastern anglers.

BODY LENGTH	10 to 12mm
HOOK	Mustad #38941, 3X Long, Size 12 to 14 Mustad #3906B, Size 8 to 10
THREAD	Brown, prewaxed 6/0
TAILS	Three medium-brown fibers from cock pheasant center tail, one body length

ABDOMEN	Dark-brown Seal-Ex dubbing with a touch of olive
GILLS	Picked out, heavy
THORAX AND LEGS	Brown guard hairs with fur
WING CASE	Dark brown
HEAD	Brown tying thread
DUBBING FORMULA	5 parts dark-brown Seal-Ex and 1 part medium-olive fur
TINTING	Fur or latex wing case tinted

brown with Pantone #154; wingtips on the latex touched lightly with gray Pantone #404M

POTAMANTHUS NYMPH
(CRAWLER)

COMMON NAMES	Golden Drake, Cream Variant, Potamanthus Cutwing
GENUS	*Potamanthus*
SPECIES	*distinctus*

AVAILABILITY This nymph is active in Eastern and Midwestern streams in the evening hours from mid-June to past mid-August, but can be used whenever a yellow-brown nymph of its size is needed.

BODY LENGTH	15mm
HOOK	Mustad #38941 3X Long, Size 10
THREAD	Brown, prewaxed 6/0
TAILS	Three light-brown fibers from cock pheasant center tail, one-third body length
ABDOMEN	Yellow-brown Seal-Ex dubbing, reddish-brown back markings

GILLS Picked out, very long

THORAX AND Yellow-brown guard hairs
LEGS and fur

WING CASE Reddish brown, one-third
body length

HEAD Brown tying thread

DUBBING 3 parts medium brown and
FORMULA 1½ parts yellow

TINTING Fur or latex wing case tinted
brown with Pantone #154M; tips on the latex
case are touched slightly with gray Pantone
#404M; back markings are applied with the
same Pantone as used for tinting the wing case

STENONEMA NYMPH
(CLINGER)

The dressing pattern and other related information pertaining to this important fly were
covered earlier in this chapter and need not be
repeated. However, I should like to include an
old wet fly of traditional vintage which has
undoubtedly undergone some changes since it
was devised: the Gold-Ribbed Hare's Ear. Its
classification could easily be that of an "all-
purpose" wet fly that, dressed in different
sizes, can be fished all year round with good
success.

GOLD-RIBBED HARE'S
EAR WET FLY

HOOK Mustad #3906B, Size 12 to
16
Mustad #39041 3X Long,
Size 10 to 12

THREAD Black, prewaxed 6/0

TAILS Ginger hen hackle fibers

BODY Brownish-gray hare's mask
dressed tapered but rough,
ribbed with narrow gold
tinsel

HACKLE A soft grouse or brown partridge body hackle; or
picked-out fur and guard
hairs from the body (on
smaller sizes or if grouse or
partridge is not available in
the required sizes, the fibers
can be tied in as a beard,
with a smaller bunch tied in
on top and sides to com-
plete the "collar")

WING Brown mottled turkey-wing
quill sections, tied
downwing

SULPHUR NYMPH
(SPRAWLER)

COMMON Little Marryatt, Pale
NAMES Evening Dun

GENUS *Ephemerella*

SPECIES *dorothea*

AVAILABILITY This fly is well known to
Eastern and Western anglers and has enjoyed a
generous amount of publicity over the years.
The fish seem to be more fond of the emerger
type of artificial, and at times trout will completely ignore the freshly hatched dun and
feed on the emerging nymph on the surface.
The Little Marryatt wet fly, for which I have
also included the dressing, or the Sulphur
Nymph, with the wing-case fur left long and
unlacquered, both work well. The emerger
nymph version must be treated with some silicone grease such as Gehrke's Gink.

BODY LENGTH	7 to 9mm	
HOOK	Mustad #3906B, Size 14 to 16	
THREAD	Brown, prewaxed 6/0	
TAILS	Three pale-tan fibers from cock pheasant center tail or wood duck flank fibers, one-half body length	
ABDOMEN	Yellowish-brown Seal-Ex dubbing	
GILLS	Picked out, lightly	
THORAX AND LEGS	Tan guard hairs with fur	
WING CASE	Brown (if made with feather case, use brown mottled turkey-wing quill section)	
HEAD	Brown tying thread	
DUBBING FORMULA	1 part reddish brown, 1 part yellow, and 3 parts cream	
TINTING	Fur or latex wing case tinted with brown Pantone #154M; wingtips on the latex touched lightly with gray Pantone #404M	

LITTLE MARRYATT
WET FLY

HOOK	Mustad #3906B, Size 16
THREAD	White, prewaxed 6/0
TAILS	Pale-ginger hackle fibers
BODY	Yellowish-tan fur dubbing
HACKLE	Pale-ginger hen hackle, soft
WING	Pale-gray duck-wing quill sections, tied downwing
HEAD	White tying thread
DUBBING FORMULA	2 parts yellow and 1 part tan fur

CRUSTACEANS

Crustaceans are not, of course, close relatives of mayflies. However, I choose to include a couple of crustacean imitations in this chapter, because the patterns are nymphlike.

CRESS BUG

COMMON NAME	Sowbug
GENUS	Representative dressing
AVAILABILITY	Found all year among the elodea in limestone streams.
BODY LENGTH	6 to 12mm
HOOK	Mustad #3906, Size 16 to 18 Mustad #3906B, Size 12 to 14
THREAD	Olive, prewaxed 6/0
BODY	Gray fur with guard hairs dyed medium olive, spun in a loop "chenille style," then wound and trimmed on top, bottom, and sides to a very flat, oval-shaped body
HEAD	Olive tying thread

FRESHWATER SHRIMP

COMMON NAME	Yellow scud
GENUS	Representative dressing
AVAILABILITY	Same as cress bug above
BODY LENGTH	9 to 12mm

HOOK   Mustad #3906B, Size 10 to 16

THREAD   Olive, prewaxed 6/0

BODY   Yellowish-olive dyed fur with guard hairs spun in a loop "chenille style," then wound and trimmed on top and both sides, leaving the fur and guard hairs long on the underside to represent the legs

HEAD   Olive tying thread

5
Mayfly Duns and Spinners

The delicate insects of the mayfly order, the Ephemeroptera, do not distinguish themselves by being particularly colorful and will appear to the naked eye in rather subdued shades ranging from dark mahogany to pale pastels in olive green and pink. Their graceful anatomy, however, has made them the primary target for fly-tyers with enough ambition and desire to create artificials that in appearance are extremely realistic-looking. Unfortunately, the most beautiful mayfly masterpieces often fail to meet the most important requirement—namely, the ability to float in a desirable manner when presented to the fish.

In my own effort to create a series of artificials possessing the most important characteristics of the natural insect, such as silhouette, translucency, and floatability, it became necessary to incorporate materials and tying methods rarely used. I do not mean to be disrespectful of the old

masters or traditional fly-dressing procedures, but a little rule-bending has resulted in very realistic-looking dry-fly imitations that are fishable, durable, and extremely effective, and, perhaps best of all, they can be dressed by anyone who has mastered the fundamentals of fly-dressing.

While my love for creative fly dressings may seem to take priority in most of my work, it would be an unforgivable sin to dismiss the beautiful traditionals that have laid the foundation for fly-tying through generations. Although they are not dealt with technically in this book, they are far from forgotten, and traditional patterns of note are mentioned with each of my dressings. For that reason it seems appropriate to make reference to important books of late: Ken Bay's *How to Tie Freshwater Flies* (Winchester Press, 1974), an excellent beginner's book; and my own

Mayfly adult

Dressing Flies for Fresh and Salt Water (Freshet Press, 1973), which deals with fly dressing for the beginner as well as the advanced tyer and, in the spirit of tradition, leads the reader step by step through all phases of modern and traditional dressing methods.

DRESSING THE MAYFLY DUN, STEP BY STEP

In the adult, whether we are concerned about the dun (subimago) or spinner (imago) stage, one mayfly doesn't differ much from another; at least for the purpose of tying and presenting the artificial to the fish, they are alike, and only the color, size, and type of material used is of concern. The three versions of dun dressings in this section can be tied by using the step-by-step instructions that follow.

Before getting started one would do well to study mayfly anatomy and get acquainted with the proportions and shapes and at the same time look into the material needed. As the anatomy drawing of the natural insect suggests, it's unmistakably one of the most beautiful insects found along the stream, one that is easy to identify by its shape. It is also deadly as a well-dressed artificial.

I have chosen *Isonychia* as the model for the instructions on how to dress all three versions, first because it's best not to work with the small flies at the outset of learning something new, and second because I am personally very fond of this large smoky-winged insect, which has given me much pleasure and enjoyment in taking some of my best "twilight fish."

The dry flies an angler decides to use, however, are a matter of personal choice, although he usually will choose those he has had good luck with and stick to them until something better comes along. The fish may not have any choice in this matter, but seem to be fooled as readily by a fly that floats on its fur body as by a traditional fly that floats on its hackle and has a fragile quill body and wood duck wings. I suppose it is fair to say that despite joining the "parachute hackle" fraternity, I still enjoy the dressing of traditional dries with the stiff natural hackles that are so hard to get—except perhaps in Harry Darbee's back yard. The most practical way of overcoming the difficulty of obtaining good stiff hackles for dry flies is

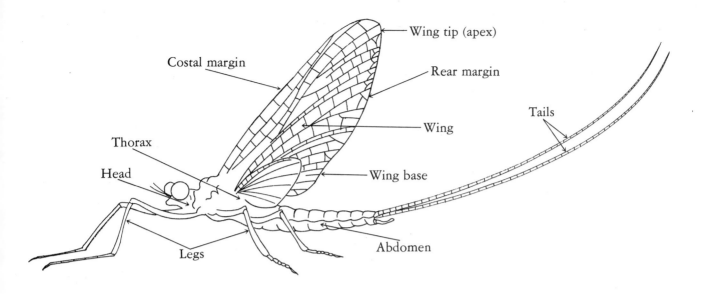

Anatomy of mayfly adult

to alter the design so the fly does not depend on its hackle to float. Then one can merely use a "fairly good" hackle wound directly around the wing to represent legs and stabilize the fly in natural upright position. The ones I have been using for years could easily be referred to as "three-in-one flies," dressed as a hair-wing for those who don't care to spend too much time at the vise, or as a cut-wing dun or realistic cut-wing for the angler who demands the ultimate in realism and delicacy and is willing to give great patience and devotion to the art.

ISONYCHIA DUN

COMMON NAMES	Dun Variant, White-Gloved Howdy, Leadwing Coachman
GENUS	*Isonychia*
SPECIES	*bicolor, sadleri*

TIME OF APPEARANCE Late afternoon and early evening from late May through August; East and Midwest

HAIR-WING DRESSING

HOOK	Mustad #94842, Size 10
THREAD	Olive, prewaxed 6/0
WINGS	Darkest-gray deer body hair; length, 16mm
TAILS	Ginger hackle fibers, same length as the wings
BODY	Dark-reddish-brown fur dubbing, fine-textured
HACKLE	Dark-ginger cock hackle, tied parachute
HEAD	Olive tying thread
DUBBING FORMULA	4 parts medium brown, 2 parts black, and 1 part red

CUT-WING DRESSING

(Same dressing as above, except for wing)

WINGS	Two dark-blue dun rooster body feathers trimmed to shape; length, 16mm

REALISTIC DRESSING

BODY LENGTH	16mm
HOOK	Mustad #94842, Size 12
THREAD	Olive, prewaxed 6/0
EXTENSION	Mahogany-brown spade hackle with fibers drawn reversed and set in Silicone Seal; length, 8mm
TAILS	Two fibers from extension material; length, 16mm

WINGS	Same as cut-wing dressing
THORAX	Fur dubbing (same as hair-wing body); length, 8mm
HACKLE	Same as hair-wing
HEAD	Same as hair-wing

Proportions

Before starting to dress these types of dry flies it should be noted that the proportions are somewhat different from those suggested for the traditionals. In the traditionals, the wings, tails, and body are of the same approximate size. The reason for the difference is simply to minimize the hook size, particularly for some of the larger artificials where the total body length would require extremely large hooks and thus affect their floating ability. The body length for hair-wing and cut-wing patterns is determined by the hook size that has been selected, which in some cases makes the fur body somewhat shorter than that of the natural—a circumstance that doesn't seem to decrease the effectiveness of the flies. The most important feature on a dry fly of this type is the wing length, which is why wing length is indicated in each pattern. The tails, while considered of minor importance on flies that float in their fur body, are the same length as the wings, unless otherwise indicated, and might well compensate for the lack in body length by suggesting the abdomen portion because of their raised position. The proportions may confuse you in the beginning and I suggest you make some small scale cards for the measurements most frequently used for the flies you will be tying. Realistic dressings have no body-length restrictions; they are made to closely coincide with the natural, as you will see in the instructions that follow.

Dressing the Hair-Wing Isonychia Dun

1. Cover the hook shank with tying thread as a foundation before taking it to where the wing is tied in, one-third of a hook length from the eye. Cut a small bunch of deer body hair from the skin and align the tips, using a funnel as explained in Chapter 2. The amount of hair needed depends on the size fly being dressed, but in this case it is about the diameter of a round toothpick when compressed lightly. Tie it in on top of the hook with the tips pointing forward over the eye. It is best to keep it on top if possible; it may flare a little, and if so, don't worry. A little flare is unavoidable. Now hold the butt ends firmly while you take several very tight turns of thread to the left, binding and compressing a small portion of the fibers to the hook shank.

2. Trim the butt ends to a long taper and wind your tying thread over them, forming a smooth, even underbody. Now take the tying thread forward to just behind the wing. Grasp all the fibers and hold them back while taking several turns of thread in front. Take some turns directly around the wing and build up a little pile of thread up the wing for a distance. There should be enough room between the uppermost windings on the wing and the hook shank to serve as a base for winding the hackle after the fur body has been applied. To keep the wing upright, take the turns directly around the wing first, then hold the thread parallel with the top of the shank, pulling lightly to the rear. When the wing sits in the desired position, spiral the thread around the shank, thus anchoring the wing in a perfect upright position. Apply some clear cement on the thread windings.

Mayfly
Duns and
Spinners
73

5-3 Step 3.

5-4 Step 4.

3. Tie in six to eight hackle fibers for the tail, which should be the same length as the wing. Do this in the same manner as if you were dressing a traditional dry fly. When they are secured, take several turns of thread directly around all the fibers, then raise them to a 45-degree angle and hold them there while pulling the thread tight and winding it around the shank, thus holding them in that position in the

same way as when securing the wing. Apply some clear cement on the thread windings. Wind the thread to directly in front of the wing and tie in the hackle; the hackle should be pointing forward with the shiny side up.

4. Apply the fur body in regular dry-fly style. It should be dubbed to just behind the wing before taking one turn close to

5-5 Step 5, the finished *Isony-chia* dun imitation.

5-6 Front view of the hair-wing dun with center wing fibers trimmed to give the impression of divided wings.

the front of the wing. Now hold the hackle to the rear and dub the front portion.

5. Wind the hackle parachute-style directly around the base of the wing, making sure that each succeeding turn is beneath the previous one. Tie off in front and cut the surplus before winding a small head.

The fly can be left as it is with just a bunched upright wing, but if you wish, you can carefully trim away the center portion and create a divided and less dense set of wings (see Fig. 5-6). When the fibers are cut away, I often apply some clear cement on the stumps and base of the wing fibers themselves for more strength.

Mayfly
Duns and
Spinners
75

5-7 Making the wings for the cut-wing *Isonychia* dun, Step 1.

5-8 Step 2.

Dressing the Cut-Wing Isonychia Dun

Anglers will generally agree that the fly requirements for slow-moving pools and long, placid stretches of stream are very rigid and only flies that closely resemble the naturals are going to fool the fish. The importance of the wings on dry flies should not be taken lightly; it is my opinion that they are the most dominating feature on a well-designed artificial. I doubt if any other fly wings look more natural than those cut to shape from the delicate body feathers of a rooster or hen, and they are surprisingly durable.

Many of my angling friends have often objected to the wings and claim that they spin on the leader tippet. However, in most cases it is not the fault of the fly, but of a wrongly selected tippet. By observing the simple rule of dividing the hook size by three, you will arrive at the correct "X" number for your tippet and thus eliminate the possibility of spinning. But as you should know, even an oversized tippet can't prevent spinning if the wings are not set straight, and I strongly recommend that you take plenty of time to learn the method of setting the wings.

The difference between the hair-wing and the cut-wing appears to be a minor

5-9   Step 3.

5-10   Step 4.

one, as only the wing makes the difference between the two, and yet, the wing preparation is extremely important and may seem time-consuming at first. However, it is quite simple once you get the hang of it and learn the proportions of those you use most often. The scale cards mentioned earlier would be a great help.

CUTTING THE WINGS

1.   Select a pair of body feathers of the same size and shade. They should be firm and straight except for a small natural curvature throughout the stem.

2.   Pull off the fuzz and lower fibers and leave only enough on the stem for the size wing you are cutting (in this case 16mm). The lowest fibers on each side of the stem must be directly across from each other.

3.   Mark the wing length on a small piece of cardboard with a pencil line, as suggested. Place the feather on the cardboard with the lower fibers directly at the pencil mark. Trim away the tip portion of both feathers, one at a time, and you have the total wing length.

4.   Hold the feather shiny side up and trim the rear margin (rear edge) to shape with a pair of large toenail clippers.

Mayfly Duns and Spinners
77

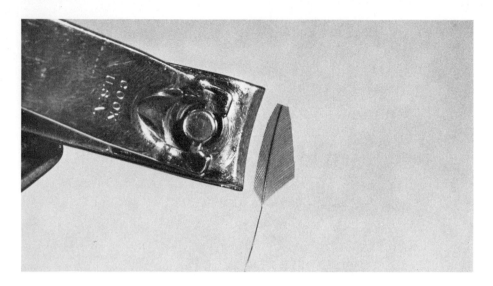

5-11 Step 5.

5-12 Step 6, cut wings ready to attach.

5. Turn the feather over and trim the costal margin (front edge). (Note that it is trimmed closer to the stem in the front, offsetting it from the center for better balance.)

6. Make a second wing in the same manner, but hold the feather with the dull underside up when cutting the rear margin. Round the corners of the apex and rear margin at the wing base, and you have the two finished wings ready to be tied in. If cut correctly, the wider portion of the wings should project toward the rear when placed on the hook with their shiny sides together.

ATTACHING AND POSITIONING THE CUT WINGS

If anything is of importance on this type of fly, it is fastening the cut wings. They must be secured with the fibers running absolutely parallel to the hook shank and sitting straight up in relation to the hook bend when viewed from the front. This may be troublesome at first, but I can assure you that there is no sense in finishing a fly that will spin like a propeller. The trick is to secure the wing stems side by side on top of the hook, then quickly raise both wings at the same time and actually

5-13 Attaching cut wings, Step 1.

5-14 Step 2.

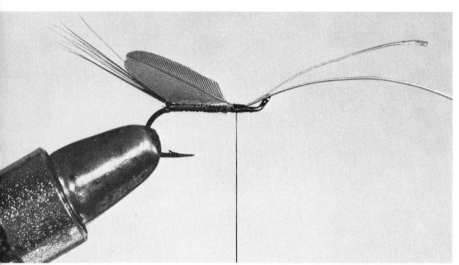

kink the stems so that the wings stay almost straight up by themselves. When this is accomplished they are held together with several turns of tying thread directly around the small portion of bare upright wing stems.

1. On this version the tail is tied in first, but in the same manner as explained for the hair-wing version. When properly set, wind the thread to a position one-third of a hook length from the eye, where the wings will be tied in. Apply a small amount of clear cement on the windings at the tail to affix it permanently.

2. Hold the wings between your fingertips with the shiny sides together and perfectly aligned with one another. Straddle the hook shank with your fingertips and place the wings on top with the stems projecting forward over the eye. Take a couple of quick turns over the stems to hold them. Now adjust the wings so that there is a bit of clear stem between the lowest fibers and the first thread windings. (The small distance is for application of hackle legs later on.) Now secure the wing stems firmly on top of the hook shank. The stems are still on in the photographs; before proceeding, cut them just short of the hook eye.

Mayfly
Duns and
Spinners
79

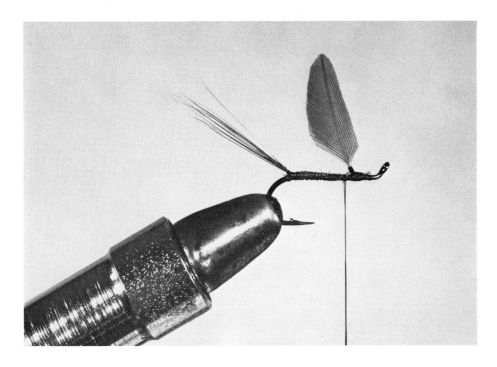

5-15 Step 3.

5-16a Step 4.

3. Raise the wings together and secure them in an upright position with windings directly around the upright wing stems and the hook shank. Apply some clear cement on the windings.

4. Make sure wings are positioned properly. See three-quarter and front views of properly set wings in Fig. 5-16.

5. The fly is now completed in the same manner as explained for the hair-wing dressing, Steps 3, 4, and 5.

The Realistic Dressing

Realistic imitations of mayflies have never been fully explored, but I suspect the fu-

5-16b   Step 4.

5-17   The finished cut-wing *Isonychia* dun, completed as for the hair-wing.

ture will bring many fine innovative tying methods that will achieve the ultimate in fly design. At present there are but a few that can qualify as practical dressings; instead they sit safely on their mounts in a frame, well out of reach of slimy fish and greedy anglers who might dare to fish with them if given a chance. As a prizefighter watches his weight, the fly-dresser must watch the weight of his artificials if they are to float on the surface as intended. The extra load of an extension may be too much, and the fly will be tail-heavy; or it is too fragile and will take but one fish before it is torn and useless.

The most practical method of forming the abdomen extension for realistic flies was discovered in the late 1950s when

Mayfly
Duns and
Spinners
81

Harry Darbee, the celebrated American fly-dresser of Livingston Manor, New York, discovered the "reverse-fiber" method: A single feather is held by the tip, and the rest of the fibers are pulled in reverse and crowded together closely along the stem, then set in lacquer to hold them in place. Harry generously let me use his method, which I wrote about in my book *Dressing Flies for Fresh and Salt Water*, and since then I have designed a list of dressings (Harry might have done the same if Elsie had locked him in his study). These patterns are fishable, durable, and not too difficult for the moderately accomplished tyer.

MAKING THE ABDOMEN EXTENSION

Almost any hackle or body feather can be used for preparing the extension, but the feather I prefer is a rooster spade hackle, because it usually has a nice webby portion on the lower end and good stiff fibers in the tip section for the tails. In some cases it is hard to locate hackles with the necessary characteristics in color and size for a particular pattern, and some tinting may be called for, either by dying the feather or by touching it up with a Pantone waterproof marking pen.

Forming the abdomen extension is by far the most difficult task in tying realistic mayflies. For a long time I struggled to find a method that was both practical and quick. Since regular fly-tying head cement is very thin, I didn't find it suitable as an adhesive for binding the fibers together, and for a long time I used clear nail polish, which is much thicker and dries fairly quickly. Unfortunately, nail polish makes the extension very stiff, and it wears off after a while. By trial and error, I found that a clear super rubber glue called G. E. Silicone Seal (made by General Electric, Silicone Products Dept., Waterford, New York) was just what I was looking for. It is a rather thick, clear, and sticky substance that comes in a tube like toothpaste. It takes very little glue to form the extension, and while it may seem a bit messy to work with, the reward is a flexible and indestructible structure that is well worth the mess. If used sparingly it adds almost no weight to the finished extension.

1. For the *Isonychia* I have selected a mahogany-colored spade hackle with tip fibers of the same length as indicated in the dressing for tails (16mm). Stroke down the fibers below the tip section and pull them off on each side, leaving the rest on a 15mm portion on the stem as shown. (This measurement changes in relation to the size extension you are making.) The fibers nearest to the tip must be directly across from one another.

2. Take a small amount of silicone glue, about what you see on the end of the dubbing needle, and apply it on the stem as seen.

5-18 Making the abdomen extension for the *Isonychia* realistic, Step 1.

5-19 Step 2.

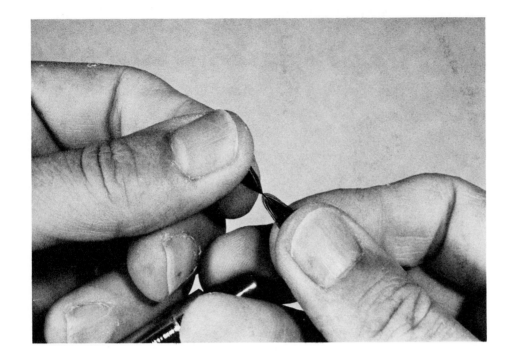

5-20 Step 3.

5-21 Step 4.

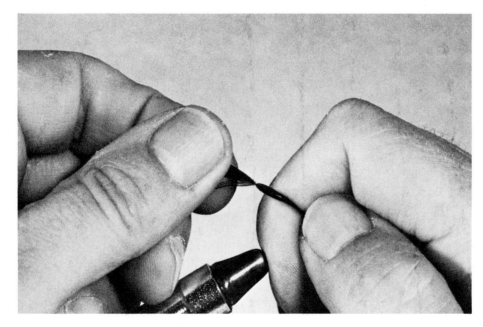

3. Hold the feather by the tip portion and draw it repeatedly out between your thumb and first finger. This will hold the fibers in reverse close to the stem. The extension will now appear to be rather flat with merely a natural curve.

4. The compressed fibers must be drawn into final shape while the glue is still tacky. To do this, I place it in the first joint of my index finger with the dull side of the feather down and my thumb on top keeping it in place. (That, incidentally, is why you have a first joint on your index finger, just in case you didn't know.) Bend your index finger slightly and draw the feather out slowly as many times as needed. This will fold the compressed

5-22a Step 5, abdomen extension ready to attach.

5-22b Step 5.

fibers down a little on each side of the stem and form V-shaped extension.

5. See Fig. 5-22 for side and top views of the finished extension. Get the extension to look like this, then lay it aside for an hour or so, till the glue has set enough for you to work with it again. In the meantime, make a couple of extra extensions, for practice or for use on additional flies later. The first couple of extensions you make may not be to your liking, and the tip may break or the fibers be pulled off while drawing them into shape, but you will soon get the hang of it and learn to apply just the right amount of pressure. When you get going it takes but a few minutes to make a half-dozen extensions.

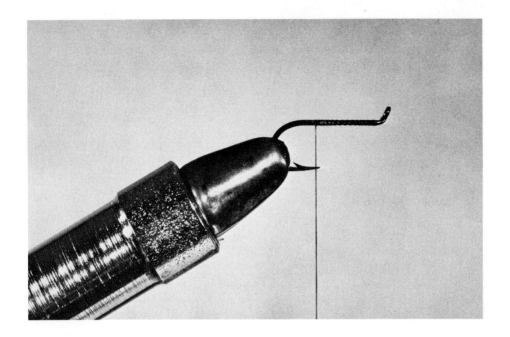

5-23 Step 6.

5-24 Step 7.

6. Wind the tying thread to a position directly above the point of the hook. (Remember, the hook for realistics is smaller than for the other two versions.) This is the tie-in point of the extension and must be positioned accurately.

7. Before the extension is tied in, it must be cut to length, which is the same as the distance between the tie-in position and the front of the hook eye, plus enough fiber and stem to fasten it on the hook. (In this case, it would be about an extra 3mm, or approximately ⅛ inch.) Apply a drop of clear cement on the hook and set the extension on top with the V-shape straddling the shank. Fasten it securely with tying thread and make sure it's sitting straight and parallel with the hook shank

5-25a Step 8.

5-25b Step 8.

horizontally, and with the hook bend vertically.

8. Separate the outer fiber on each side of the tip portion and hold them out of the way while trimming out the center portion. Do not trim too close, but leave a bit of stump between the tails so that you can apply a little silicone glue. This is best applied by first rubbing it between your fingers and then applying it as you would silicone dry-fly flotant. When it is applied, draw it on the tail fibers also. This strengthens the tail structure. If a three-tail abdomen is needed, just leave two fibers on one side and one on the other. The third one can be centered when the silicone has been applied, then kept centered while drying.

FINISHING THE REALISTIC DRESSING

The abdomen extension must be fairly dry and well set before continuing the dressing. I have found it convenient to complete several abdomens and attach them to the hooks at the same time. Not only will you always need more than just one fly, but as you get into the swing of making the extensions, each one seems to get better than the preceding ones. The steps needed for completion of the Realistic Mayfly have already been explained in the instructions for the hair-wing and cut-wing, so they need not be repeated here. When applying the fur body, or thorax as it is called on the realistic, care must be taken to start the dubbing at the abdomen tie-in point and cover the thread windings. Start the dubbing procedure sparsely and make a smooth transition between the abdomen fibers and the thorax fur. The finished realistic imitation is shown in Fig. 5-26.

SIMPLIFIED ABDOMEN EXTENSION

There are times when the regular abdomen extension made with fibers drawn into shape is not practical, particularly on very small flies or when weight must be kept to an absolute minimum. For these occasions the simplified one might work better and is much simpler to make.

The characteristics of the feathers used are the same, but instead of drawing the fibers into shape, they are trimmed off, leaving only some small stumps that can then be set in silicone glue. (See Fig. 5-27.) When the glue is applied it is drawn through the fingers, holding it by the stem, thus setting the short fibers in the direction of the tail rather than reversed like the one previously explained. It should be noted that the trimming must be done in such a way that there is enough fiber left to make an extension that is wide enough for the particular insect you are copying. The simplified extension is by no means inferior but does not have the "full" look of the other one. While the regular type is better for most realistic dun dressings, the simplified type is by far better for the large spinners described later.

DRESSING THE MAYFLY SPINNER, STEP BY STEP

The spinners, or imagos as the entomologists call them, are the last stage in the life cycle of a mayfly. The insect has now changed from a rather dull-colored sub-imago to a bright, shiny spinner with almost glassy clear wings and somewhat longer tails than those of the duns. Some mayfly species change from duns to spinners almost immediately after hatching, such as those of the genera *Caenis* (*Tricorythodes*) and *Ephoron,* while others

5-26 *Above.* The finished realistic *Isonychia* dun, completed as for the hair-wing and cutwing.

5-27 Simplified abdomen extension.

Mayfly
Duns and
Spinners
89

5-28 Dressing the hair-wing
Isonychia spinner, Step 1.

ISONYCHIA SPINNER

HOOK	Mustad #94842, Size 10
THREAD	Olive, prewaxed 6/0
TAILS	Four to six ginger hackle fibers, one and one-half times body length, dressed in an open V-shape
WINGS	Pale-gray dyed deer body hair tied spent
BODY	Dark-reddish-brown fur dubbing
DUBBING FORMULA	Same as for the dun

take as long as twenty-four hours to appear in their new attire, which means that you may often observe spinners of insects from the previous day's hatching, but by no means does this handiwork of nature make any difference when fishing the artificial spinner. The main difference between dun and spinner, as far as the fly-tyer is concerned, lies in the wing position. The dun is usually upright and slightly divided, whereas the spinner is spent or half-spent when it falls into the water when it reaches the last few moments of its life.

1. Tie in the deer body hair in the same manner as you would when dressing the hair-wing dun, but omit the thread windings directly around the whole fiber bunch. Instead, divide the hair into two equal parts, one for each wing, then take a couple of criss-cross windings between them. Now take several tight windings directly around the base of each bunch separately and set them in spent-wing position. Apply some clear cement on the windings and make sure the structure is even on both sides when seen from the front, using the hook bend as a guideline.

Also determine if the wings should sit full-spent, in a line from which the hook bend will be seen at a 90-degree angle, or if each wing should be raised a little to a half-spent position. When the cement dries, the wings will sit affixed in whichever position you have chosen.

2. Apply a very small amount of fur on the tying thread and dub a small fur ball on the shank above the point of the hook barb. This fur will keep the tail fibers divided when tied in, and if kept small, will blend with the rest of the body.

Mayfly
Duns and
Spinners
91

5-30 Step 3.

5-31 Step 4.

3. Tie in one bunch of tail fibers at a time, making sure they are both of the same length. As seen in Fig. 5-30, they are laid on top and across the shank where they are fastened with a few thread windings close to the fur ball. When both tails are secured, apply a little clear ce-ment on the windings and trim away the surplus.

4. Dub the body and apply some fur at the wing and in between the criss-cross turns.

5-32 Step 5, the finished hair-wing *Isonychia* spinner imitation, front and top views.

5. Wind the dubbing on the shank in front of the wing and tie off. This finishes the spinner.

A Variation: The Extension Spinner

An interesting variation of the spinner is created by using the simplified extension that was explained earlier in the section dealing with realistic duns. It is no secret

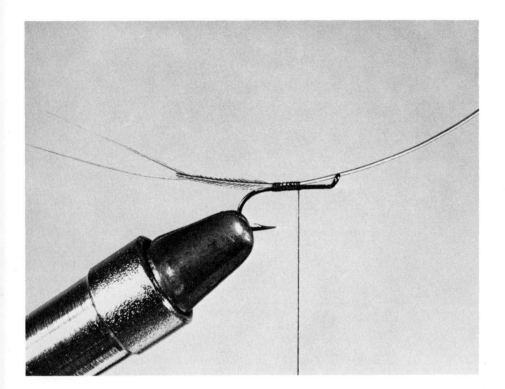

that large spinners such as those of the *Hexagenia* and *Ephemera* species have caused some problem for the fly-dresser in the past, particularly in the hook department. By using an extension the problem seems to have been overcome, and these large semi-realistic spinner types have proven to be very effective and much easier to cast than those with heavy hooks. Aside from adding the extension, the wing and thorax portion of the fly has been modified, with the wing butt ends worked into an "irresistible" type of deer-hair

thorax which is trimmed to line up with the taper of the extension. While I have used the simple extension even on small spinners with a fur thorax, I have only used the deer-hair thorax application on larger flies, but it surely offers a challenge, and by using a very fine-textured deer hair, perhaps even the smallest sizes are not out of reach.

1. Make a simplified abdomen extension and tie it in on top of a Size 12 up-eyed

hook. (Use the realistic dressing as a guide for abdomen length.) The first fibers of the extension should be located over the hook point, and the extension should lie flat and parallel with the shank.

2. Select a bunch of deer body hair that is twice as large as the one used for the regular deer-hair spinner wings and tie it in at a position one-third hook length from the eye. The best way to do this is to hold the hair firmly between your thumb

and index finger and lay it on top of the hook. Take two loose turns around the hair. (Remember, the distance between the first windings and the tip of the hair determines the wing length, in this case 16mm.) Then press it down around the hook shank and tighten the thread while holding it firmly without letting it spin by itself, which would make it almost impossible for you to separate the butts from the tips. Take several more tight turns at the same approximate place as the first ones to firmly secure the hair.

Mayfly
Duns and
Spinners
95

5-35 Step 3.

5-36 Step 4.

3. Trim the butt ends to a taper all the way around the shank. The hairs closest to the hook shank should reach a little beyond the hook bend, while the rest get shorter as they are tapered to close behind the wing.

4. Spiral the tying thread slowly through the hair back to the beginning of the ex-tension. Make sure to pull each turn tight to flare the hair. Now spiral it back to close behind the wing without winding the hair under. This will form a hair body much like that of the irresistible dry fly, or the head on a Muddler Minnow. Trim the hair thorax so it looks like a continuation of the abdomen, including trimming of wingtip hair *below* the hook shank.

5-37 Step 5.

5-38 Step 6, the finished hair-wing spinner with simplified extension.

5. Grasp all the wing hairs and pull them upright, and hold them while taking some thread windings in front to keep it up. Separate the hair into three bunches. The ones on the side should contain enough hair to form the wings.

6. Trim away the center portion of hair to form the top of the thorax before set-ting the wings in spent position with windings directly around their base. Do not criss-cross between them or you will ruin the thorax. Apply some clear cement at each wing base and on top of the thorax. The empty space in front of the wing is filled in with a little fur dubbing to match the rest of the body and the Deer Hair Spinner is finished.

Mayfly
Duns and
Spinners
97

5-39 A tiny Caenis spinner hair-wing imitation, on the end of a paper match. The white abdomen and black thorax are for the female dressing.

5-40 *Opposite.* Bob Stearns of Miami fooled this handsome brown with a Caenis hair-wing spinner on a small Pennsylvania limestone stream. The fish lost only its pride; Bob released it.

Since the wing is what determines the color hair to use, the thorax may not match the color of the abdomen. This can be corrected by tinting the thorax with a Pantone Marker. Admittedly, it may take a few tries before you can correctly estimate the amount of hair needed, but if you are willing to practice, your efforts will be rewarded with a very durable and effective spinner—one that can perhaps be built upon with ideas of your own.

SELECTED MAYFLY DUN AND SPINNER DRESSINGS

The dressings included in the list that follows are those most frequently used in different parts of the country, at least by me and by many of the more knowledgeable fishing friends who give me the pleasure of sharing a piece of water now and then, who are always first to admit the impossibility of selecting a conclusive list

of dressings that work every time everywhere, and who are also first to admit that if failure strikes, I probably dressed their fly.

To those who have favorite flies not found on the list, I apologize, but perhaps the preceding tying instructions will enable them to proceed on their own and establish new dressings that we all someday may enjoy.

You will note that in the dressing patterns spinner tails are often mentioned as being tied "straight back." This alternate method works for all spinners and is merely an ordinary traditional dry-fly tail arrangement.

BLUE-WINGED HENDRICKSON DUN

COMMON NAMES	Lady Beaverkill, Red Quill, Hendrickson
GENUS	*Ephemerella*
SPECIES	*subvaria*

TIME OF APPEARANCE Second week of April through May on Eastern and Midwestern streams, starting in early afternoon

HAIR-WING DRESSING

HOOK	Mustad #94842, Size 12 to 14
THREAD	Tan, prewaxed 6/0
WINGS	Dark-gray deer body hair tips; wings: 13mm long
TAILS	Small bunch of wood duck fibers; tails: 12mm long
BODY	Creamish-pink fur dubbing

HACKLE	Medium-blue-dun rooster hackle, tied parachute
HEAD	Tan tying thread
DUBBING FORMULA	In lieu of the urine-stained fur from a vixen, the darkest cream fox belly fur with medium pink added to give it a pinkish cast is acceptable

CUT-WING DRESSING

(Same as hair-wing except wings)

WINGS	Two medium-blue-dun rooster body feathers trimmed to size; wings: 13mm long

REALISTIC DRESSING

BODY LENGTH	12mm
HOOK	Mustad #94842, Size 14
THREAD	Tan, prewaxed 6/0
EXTENSION	Small wood duck flank feather (light-colored) with fibers drawn reversed and set in silicone glue; extension: 6mm long; when extension is tied in, tint it lightly with pink Pantone #162M
TAILS	Three fibers from extension material; tails: 12mm long
WINGS	Same as cut-wing
THORAX	Fur dubbing (same as hair-wing body); thorax: 6mm long
HACKLE	Same as hair-wing
HEAD	Same as hair-wing

Modern Fly
Dressings
for the
Practical
Angler
100

SPINNER DRESSING

HOOK	Mustad #94842, Size 12 to 14
THREAD	Brown, prewaxed 6/0
WINGS	Lightest-gray deer body hair tips, tied spent; wings: 13mm long
TAILS	Wood duck flank feather fibers tied open in V-shape or straight back; tails: 15mm long
BODY	Medium-reddish-brown fur dubbing
HEAD	Brown tying thread
DUBBING FORMULA	2 parts medium brown, 1 part black, and 1 part red

TRADITIONAL DRESSING (RED QUILL)

HOOK	Mustad #94833, Size 12 to 14
THREAD	Black, prewaxed 6/0
TAILS	Medium-blue-dun hackle fibers
WINGS	Wood duck flank feather
BODY	Reddish-brown hackle stem, stripped
HACKLE	Medium-blue-dun rooster hackles
HEAD	Black tying thread

DARK LEPTOPHLEBIA DUN

COMMON NAMES	Black Quill, Whirling Dun
GENUS	*Leptophlebia*
SPECIES	*cupida*

TIME OF APPEARANCE In the late morning through the afternoon from late April through May in the East and Midwest

HAIR-WING DRESSING

HOOK	Mustad #94842, Size 10 to 12
THREAD	Black, prewaxed 6/0
WINGS	Darkest-gray-brown deer body hair tips; wings: 14mm long
TAILS	Dark-brown hackle fibers; tails: 15mm long
BODY	Dark-reddish-brown fur dubbing
HACKLE	Coch-y-bondhu rooster hackle, tied parachute
HEAD	Black tying thread
DUBBING FORMULA	3 parts dark brown and 1 part red

CUT-WING DRESSING

(Same as hair-wing except wings)

WINGS	Dark-rusty-blue-dun hen hackle or body feather (this can also be a dark-ginger-dyed blue dun if natural is not available) trimmed to shape; wings: 14mm long

REALISTIC DRESSING

BODY LENGTH	14mm
HOOK	Mustad #94842, Size 12
THREAD	Black, prewaxed 6/0
EXTENSION	Coch-y-bondhu spade hackle or webby neck hackle from rooster or hen,

with fibers drawn reversed
and set in silicone glue; extension: 7mm long

TAILS   Three fibers from extension
material, center tail trimmed
a little shorter than the
outer ones; tails: 15mm long

WINGS   Same as cut-wing

THORAX   Fur dubbing (same as hair-
wing body); thorax: 7mm
long

HACKLE   Same as hair-wing

HEAD   Same as hair-wing

SPINNER DRESSING

HOOK   Mustad #94842, Size 10 to
12

THREAD   Black, prewaxed 6/0

WINGS   Medium-gray deer body
hair tips, tied spent; wings:
14mm long

TAILS   Brown hackle fibers tied
open V-shape or straight-
back; tails: 17mm long

BODY   Dark-reddish-brown dubbing

HEAD   Black tying thread

DUBBING   Same as for the hair-wing
FORMULA   dressing

TRADITIONAL DRESSING
(BLACK QUILL)

HOOK   Mustad #94833, Size 10 to
12

THREAD   Black, prewaxed 6/0

Modern Fly
Dressings
for the
Practical
Angler
102

TAILS   Blackish-blue-dun hackle
fibers

WINGS   Black hackle tips

BODY   Badger hackle stem,
stripped

HACKLE   Blackish-blue-dun rooster
hackles

HEAD   Black tying thread

GOLDEN DRAKE DUN

COMMON   Evening Dun, Cream
NAMES   Variant

GENUS   *Potamanthus*

SPECIES   *distinctus*

TIME OF APPEARANCE   At twilight on Eastern and Midwestern streams, from mid-June to
the first week of August

HAIR-WING DRESSING

HOOK   Mustad #94842, Size 10 to
12

THREAD   Yellow, prewaxed 6/0

WINGS   Pale-yellow-dyed deer body
hair tips; wings: 16mm long

TAILS   Pale-yellow hackle fibers;
tails: 16mm long

BODY   Pale-yellow fur dubbing

HACKLE   Palest ginger rooster hackle,
tied parachute

HEAD   Yellow tying thread

DUBBING   Equal amounts of yellow
FORMULA   and creamy white

CUT-WING DRESSING

(Same as hair-wing except wings)

WINGS   Palest-yellow-dyed rooster body feather or hen neck hackle trimmed to shape; wings: 16mm long

REALISTIC DRESSING

BODY LENGTH   16mm

HOOK   Mustad #94842, Size 12

THREAD   Yellow, prewaxed 6/0

EXTENSION   Palest-yellow-dyed spade hackle with fibers drawn reversed and set in silicone glue; extension: 8mm long

TAILS   Three fibers from the extension material; tails: 16mm long

WINGS   Same as cut-wing

THORAX   Fur dubbing (same as for the hair-wing body); thorax: 8mm long

HACKLE   Same as for hair-wing

HEAD   Same as for hair-wing

GOLDEN SPINNER DRESSING

HOOK   Mustad #94842, Size 10 to 12

THREAD   Yellow, prewaxed 6/0

WINGS   Palest-gray deer body hair tips tied spent; wings: 16mm long

TAILS   Pale-yellow hackle fibers tied open V-shape or

straight back; tails: 18mm long

BODY   Pale-yellow fur dubbing (same as hair-wing dun)

HEAD   Yellow tying thread

TRADITIONAL DRESSING (CREAM VARIANT)

HOOK   Mustad #94833, Size 10 to 12

THREAD   Yellow, prewaxed 6/0

TAILS   Cream hackle fibers, very stiff and fairly long

WINGS   None

BODY   Cream hackle stem, stripped

HACKLE   Cream rooster neck or saddle hackle

HEAD   Yellow tying thread

GREEN DRAKE DUN (EASTERN)

COMMON NAMES   Green Drake, Coffin Fly

GENUS   *Ephemera*

SPECIES   *guttulata*

TIME OF APPEARANCE   Last days of May through the first weeks of June, sporadically throughout the day and early evening hours

HAIR-WING DRESSING

HOOK   Mustad #94842, Size 10

THREAD   Yellow, prewaxed 6/0

WINGS   Well-marked grayish-brown deer body hair tips; wings: 22mm long

TAILS	Three dark moose mane fibers; tails same length as wings
BODY	Pale-creamish-yellow fur dubbing with an olive cast
HACKLE	Golden badger rooster hackle, tied parachute
HEAD	Yellow tying thread
DUBBING FORMULA	3 parts creamy white, 1 part yellow with a pinch of medium olive to give an olive cast

CUT-WING DRESSING

(Same as hair-wing except for wings)

WINGS	Two wood duck flank feathers, or two well-marked mallard flank feathers dyed chartreuse, trimmed to shape; wings: 22mm long

REALISTIC DRESSING

BODY LENGTH	22mm
HOOK	Mustad #94842, Size 10
THREAD	Yellow, prewaxed 6/0
EXTENSION	Mallard flank feather dyed pale creamish-yellow with a pinch of olive added; fibers drawn reversed and set in silicone glue; optional back marking can be applied with a brown Pantone Marker; extension: 11mm long
TAILS	Three fibers from extension material; tails: 22mm long
WINGS	Same as cut-wing

THORAX	Fur dubbing (same as for hair-wing body); thorax: 11mm long
HACKLE	Same as hair-wing dressing
HEAD	Yellow tying thread

SPINNER DRESSING
(COFFIN FLY)

HOOK	Mustad #94842, Size 10
THREAD	White, prewaxed 6/0
WINGS	Well-marked gray deer body hair tips, tied spent; wings: 22mm long
TAILS	Three dark moose mane fibers tied straight back; tails: 28mm long
BODY	Creamy white fur dubbing
HEAD	White tying thread
DUBBING FORMULA	Equal parts of cream and white fur
REMARK	This spinner is a good candidate for a simplified extension made from a creamy white spade hackle. The tails are then tinted with a dark brown Pantone Marker.

TRADITIONAL DRESSING
(WHITE WULFF)

HOOK	Mustad #94833, Size 10
THREAD	White, prewaxed 6/0
TAILS	White calf tail
WINGS	White calf tail
BODY	Creamy white fur or yarn
HACKLE	Golden badger
HEAD	White tying thread

GRAY FOX DUN

COMMON
NAMES Gray Fox, Ginger Quill
GENUS *Stenonema*
SPECIES *fuscum*

TIME OF APPEARANCE Start to hatch in midmorning on some waters and late in the day on others; found in East and Midwest from mid-May through June

HAIR-WING DRESSING

HOOK	Mustad #94842, Size 12 to 14
THREAD	Yellow, prewaxed 6/0
WINGS	Well-marked grayish-brown deer body hair tips; wings: 14mm long
TAILS	Small bunch of wood duck fibers; tails: 12mm long
BODY	Yellowish-tan fur dubbing
HACKLE	One light ginger and one grizzly, wound together (a grizzly dyed light tan may be used, in which case only one hackle is needed)
HEAD	Yellow tying thread
DUBBING FORMULA	1 part medium brown, 1 part yellow, and 1 part cream

CUT-WING DRESSING

(Same as hair-wing except for wings)

WINGS	Two gray partridge body feathers trimmed to shape; wings: 14mm long

REALISTIC DRESSING

BODY LENGTH	12mm
HOOK	Mustad #94842, Size 14
THREAD	Yellow, prewaxed 6/0
EXTENSION	Pale-ginger spade hackle with fibers drawn reversed and set in silicone glue; optional back markings, brown Pantone #154M; extension: 6 mm long
TAILS	Two fibers from the extension material; tails: 12mm long
WINGS	Same as cut-wing
THORAX	Fur dubbing (same as hair-wing body; length, 6mm
HACKLE	Same as hair-wing
HEAD	Same as hair-wing

SPINNER DRESSING

HOOK	Mustad #94842, Size 12 to 14
THREAD	Yellow, prewaxed 6/0
WINGS	Lightest-gray deer body hair tips, tied spent; wings: 14mm long
TAILS	Wood duck flank feather fibers tied open V-shape or straight back; tails: 15mm long
BODY	Yellowish-amber fur dubbing
HEAD	Yellow tying thread
DUBBING FORMULA	2 parts cream, 1 part medium reddish-brown, and 1 part yellow

TRADITIONAL DRESSING
(GRAY FOX)

HOOK — Mustad #94833, Size 12 to 14

THREAD — Yellow, prewaxed 6/0

TAILS — Ginger hackle fibers

WINGS — Mallard flank feather

BODY — Light-fawn-colored fox fur

HACKLE — Light ginger and grizzly wound together

HEAD — Yellow tying thread

HAIR-WING CAENIS DUN

COMMON NAMES — Angler's Curse, Tiny White-Winged Dun

GENUS — *Tricorythodes*

SPECIES — Various

TIME OF APPEARANCE — Midmorning hours from June through September and early October; found throughout the country

HOOK — Mustad #94842, Size 22 to 28

THREAD — Black, prewaxed 6/0

TAILS — Light-blue-dun hackle fibers, dressed in an open V-shape

WINGS — Small bunch of light-gray deer body hair set upright (keep the hair bunch very sparse, using the finest-textured hair you have)

BODY — Very sparse black fur dubbing, heaviest near the wing

HACKLE — None

Modern Fly
Dressings
for the
Practical
Angler
106

REMARK — Because of its size, the hackle is omitted and the tails are tied in an open V-shape and are not raised as is customary on most of the other patterns. The outrigger type of tail construction will stabilize the fly, which in this case floats directly on its fur body with the aid of dry-fly flotant.

HAIR-WING SPINNER DRESSING

HOOK — Mustad #94842, Size 22 to 28

THREAD — Black, prewaxed 6/0

TAILS — Three light-blue-dun fibers tied straight back, fairly long

WINGS — Lightest-gray deer body hair tips, tied spent

ABDOMEN — Light moose mane hair

THORAX — Black fur dubbing

HEAD — Black tying thread

REMARK — This fly is more important in the area where I fish than the dun, but I recommend that you watch closely to determine on which the fish are feeding.

IRON BLUE DUN

COMMON NAMES — Gordon Quill, Quill Gordon, Iron Dun

GENUS — *Epeorus*

SPECIES — *pleuralis*

TIME OF APPEARANCE — Early afternoon from mid-April through May, East and Midwest

HAIR-WING DRESSING

HOOK — Mustad #94842, Size 12 to 14

THREAD	Olive, prewaxed 6/0
WINGS	Dark-gray deer body hair tips; wings: 11mm long
TAILS	Small bunch of wood duck fibers; tails same length as wings
BODY	Grayish-yellow fur dubbing
HACKLE	Rusty-blue-dun rooster hackle, tied parachute
HEAD	Olive tying thread
DUBBING FORMULA	2 parts medium brown, 2 parts yellow, and 1 part gray beaver

CUT-WING DRESSING

(Same as hair-wing except for wings)

WINGS	Two medium-blue-dun rooster body feathers trimmed to shape; wings: 11mm long

REALISTIC DRESSING

BODY LENGTH	11mm
HOOK	Mustad #94842, Size 14
THREAD	Olive, prewaxed 6/0
EXTENSION	A small wood duck flank feather with fibers drawn reversed and set in silicone glue; extension is sometimes tinted with yellow Pantone Marker #115M if too light; extension: 6mm long
TAILS	Two fibers from extension material; tails: 11mm long
WINGS	Same as cut-wing

THORAX	Fur dubbing (same as hair-wing body); thorax: 5mm long
HACKLE	Same as hair-wing
HEAD	Same as hair-wing

SPINNER DRESSING

HOOK	Mustad #94842, Size 12 to 14
THREAD	Olive, prewaxed 6/0
WINGS	Palest-grayish-tan deer body hair tips, tied spent; wings: 11mm long
TAILS	Medium-blue-dun hackle fibers tied open V-shape or straight back; tails: 15mm long
BODY	Same as hair-wing
HEAD	Olive tying thread

REMARK   Suitable for simplified extension, in which case thorax is tinted to match the ginger-colored feather used for the extension. It is best to use a Size 14 hook in this case.

TRADITIONAL DRESSING
(QUILL GORDON)

HOOK	Mustad #94833, Size 12 to 14
THREAD	Olive, prewaxed 6/0
TAILS	Medium-blue-dun hackle fibers
WINGS	Wood duck flank feather
BODY	Stripped quill from the eye of a peacock feather, bleached

HACKLE   Medium-rusty-blue-dun
          rooster hackle

LIGHT CAHILL DUN

COMMON   Ginger Quill, Cahill, Light
NAMES   Cahill

GENUS   *Stenonema*

SPECIES   *canadense, ithaca*

TIME OF APPEARANCE Hatching sporadically throughout the day on Eastern and Midwestern waters from beginning of June
through July

HAIR-WING DRESSING

HOOK   Mustad #94842, Size 12 to
          14

THREAD   Yellow, prewaxed 6/0

WINGS   Light-gray deer body hair
          tips; wings: 12mm long

TAILS   Small bunch of pale wood
          duck fibers; tails same
          length as wings

BODY   Creamish-tan fur dubbing

HACKLE   Palest ginger hackle, tied
          parachute

HEAD   Yellow tying thread

DUBBING   3 parts yellowish cream and
FORMULA   1 part light tan

CUT-WING DRESSING

(Same as hair-wing except for wings)

WINGS   Two small wood duck flank
          feathers or pale-mottled-tan
          hen neck hackle trimmed to
          shape; wings: 12mm long

REALISTIC DRESSING

BODY LENGTH   11mm

HOOK   Mustad #94842, Size 14

THREAD   Yellow, prewaxed 6/0

EXTENSION Yellowish-tan body feather
          of hen neck hackle, with
          fibers drawn reversed and
          set in silicone glue; exten-
          sion: 6mm long

TAILS   Two fibers from extension
          material; tails: 12mm long

WINGS   Same as cut-wing

THORAX   Fur dubbing (same as for
          the hair-wing body); thorax:
          5mm long

HACKLE   Same as hair-wing

HEAD   Same as hair-wing

SPINNER DRESSING

HOOK   Mustad #94842, Size 12 to
          14

THREAD   Yellow, prewaxed 6/0

WINGS   Palest-gray deer body hair
          tips, tied spent; wings:
          12mm long

TAILS   Light ginger hackle fibers
          tied open V-shape, or
          straight back; tails: 15mm
          long

BODY   Creamish-tan fur dubbing
          (use hair-wing dubbing for-
          mula)

HEAD   Yellow tying thread

TRADITIONAL DRESSING
(LIGHT CAHILL)

HOOK | Mustad #94833, Size 12 to 14

THREAD | Yellow, prewaxed 6/0

TAILS | Light-ginger hackle fibers

WINGS | Palest wood duck flank feather

BODY | Cream fur dubbing

HACKLE | Very light ginger

HEAD | Yellow tying thread

LITTLE BLUE MAYFLY

COMMON
NAMES | Blue Quill, Blue Dun

GENUS | *Paraleptophlebia*

SPECIES | *adoptiva*

TIME OF APPEARANCE From noon through the day, from mid-April through May, East and Midwest

HAIR-WING DRESSING

HOOK | Mustad #94842, Size 18 to 20

THREAD | Brown, prewaxed 6/0

WINGS | Darkest-gray deer body hair tips; wings: 7mm long

TAILS | Brown hackle fibers, same length as wings

BODY | Dark reddish brown with an olive cast

HACKLE | Medium-blue-dun rooster hackle tied parachute

HEAD | Brown tying thread

DUBBING
FORMULA | 3 parts dark brown, 1 part red, and 1 part medium olive

REMARK I sometimes use deer body hair that has been dyed dark gray for the wings, but only when it's absolutely necessary.

CUT-WING DRESSING

(Same as hair-wing except for wings)

WINGS | Darkest-blue-gray rooster body feathers trimmed to shape (for these small sizes I often use hen neck hackle instead); wings: 7mm long

REALISTIC DRESSING

BODY LENGTH | 7mm

HOOK | Mustad #94842, Size 20

THREAD | Brown, prewaxed 6/0

EXTENSION | Simplified type; dark-reddish-brown hen hackle; extension: 4mm long

TAILS | Three fibers from extension material; tails: 7mm long

WINGS | Same as cut-wing

THORAX | Fur dubbing, very sparse (same as hair-wing body)

HACKLE | Same as hair-wing

HEAD | Same as hair-wing

SPINNER DRESSING

HOOK | Mustad #94842, Size 18 to 20

THREAD | Brown, prewaxed 6/0

WINGS Palest-grayish-tan deer body hair tips, tied spent; wings: 7mm long

TAILS Pale-blue-dun hackle fibers, tied straight back; tails: 10mm long

BODY Same as for hair-wing

HEAD Brown tying thread

TRADITIONAL DRESSING (DARK RED QUILL)

HOOK Mustad #94833, Size 18

THREAD Black, prewaxed 6/0

TAILS Dark-blue-gray hackle fibers

WINGS Two dark-blue-gray hackle tips

BODY Reddish-brown hackle stem, stripped

HACKLE Very dark blue-gray dun

HEAD Black tying thread

LITTLE BLUE-WINGED BAETIS DUN

COMMON
NAME Blue-Winged Olive

GENUS *Baetis*

SPECIES Various

TIME OF APPEARANCE Throughout country from April through October

HAIR-WING DRESSING

HOOK Mustad #94842, Size 16 to 24

THREAD Olive, prewaxed 6/0

WINGS Medium-gray deer body hair tips; wings one body length long

TAILS Medium-blue-dun hackle fibers; tails same length as wings

BODY Medium-brown, or medium-olive, or medium-olive-brown fur dubbing

HACKLE Medium-blue-dun or grizzly, tied parachute

HEAD Olive tying thread

DUBBING FORMULA The first two dubbings are straight base colors; the third is equal parts of medium brown and medium olive

REMARK I sometimes omit the parachute-type hackle, and instead tie the hackle in at the tail before the body is dubbed, then spiral a few turns forward to the front and tie off (open palmer style). When hackle is applied I trim off all the fibers under the fly.

CUT-WING DRESSING

(Same as hair-wing dressing, except for wings)

WINGS Medium-blue-gray hen hackle feathers trimmed to shape, and as long as one hook length

REALISTIC DRESSING

Since we are dealing with very small artificials in this instance, it's not practical to dress a full-fledged realistic. However, some added realism can be achieved by replacing the tail fibers with a simplified extension. In that case, use one size smaller hook than intended for the regular dressing, and needless to say, they are dressed with a set of fine cut wings.

SPINNER DRESSING

HOOK	Mustad #94842, Size 16 to 24
THREAD	Olive, prewaxed 6/0
WINGS	Palest-gray deer body hair tips, finest texture, tied spent; wings one body length long
TAILS	Medium-blue-dun hackle fibers tied straight back, very stiff
BODY	Medium or dark brown, or medium reddish-brown (dark chestnut)
HEAD	Olive tying thread

LITTLE SULPHUR DUN

COMMON NAMES	Little Marryatt, Pale Evening Dun, Cut-Wing Sulphur Dun
GENUS	*Ephemerella*
SPECIES	*dorothea*

TIME OF APPEARANCE Late in the day or early evening in the East and Midwest, from middle of May to the first week of July

HAIR-WING DRESSING

HOOK	Mustad #94842, Size 16 to 18
THREAD	Yellow, prewaxed 6/0
WINGS	Medium-gray deer body hair tips; wings: 8mm long
TAILS	Light-ginger hackle fibers, same length as wings
BODY	Sulphur-yellow fur dubbing
HACKLE	Very pale ginger, tied parachute
HEAD	Yellow tying thread
DUBBING FORMULA	4 parts bright yellow, 1 part cream, and 1 part medium olive

CUT-WING DRESSING

(Same as hair-wing except for wings)

WINGS	Very-light-blue-dun body feather or hen hackle, trimmed to shape; wings: 8mm long

REALISTIC DRESSING

BODY LENGTH	8mm
HOOK	Mustad #94842, Size 18
THREAD	Yellow, prewaxed 6/0
EXTENSION	Small hen hackle or body feather dyed sulphur yellow, with fibers drawn reversed and set in silicone glue (or simplified extension of the same color); extension: 4mm long
TAILS	Three fibers from extension material; tails: 8mm long
WINGS	Same as cut-wing
THORAX	Fur dubbing (same as hair-wing body); thorax: 4mm long
HACKLE	Same as hair-wing
HEAD	Same as hair-wing

LITTLE SULPHUR SPINNER

HOOK	Mustad #94842, Size 16 to 18
THREAD	Yellow, prewaxed 6/0
WINGS	Dyed palest-gray deer body hair tips, tied spent; wings: 8mm long
TAILS	Palest-blue-dun hackle fibers tied open V-shape or straight back; tails: 12mm long
BODY	Yellowish-amber fur dubbing
HEAD	Yellow tying thread
DUBBING FORMULA	1 part chestnut brown, 1 part yellow, and 3 parts cream

TRADITIONAL DRESSING (PALE EVENING DUN)

HOOK	Mustad #94833, Size 16 to 18
THREAD	Yellow, prewaxed 6/0
TAILS	Palest-ginger hackle fibers
WINGS	Pale-blue-dun hackle tips
BODY	Creamish-yellow fur dubbing
HACKLE	Palest-ginger hackle
HEAD	Yellow tying thread
DUBBING FORMULA	Equal parts cream and yellow, fine-textured fur

MARCH BROWN DUN (AMERICAN)

COMMON NAMES	Ginger Quill, Brown Drake, March Brown
GENUS	*Stenonema*
SPECIES	*vicarium*

TIME OF APPEARANCE Sporadically during the day from mid-May through June, East and Midwest

HAIR-WING DRESSING

HOOK	Mustad #94842, Size 10 to 12
THREAD	Yellow, prewaxed 6/0
WINGS	Well-marked grayish-brown deer body hair tips; wings: 16mm long
TAILS	Small bunch of wood duck fibers; tails: 14mm long
BODY	Yellowish-amber fur dubbing
HACKLE	One grizzly and one dark ginger wound together, parachute-style (a grizzly dyed medium brown will give the same result, in which case only one hackle is used)
HEAD	Yellow
DUBBING FORMULA	2 parts cream, 1 part medium reddish-brown, and 1 part yellow

CUT-WING DRESSING

(Same as hair-wing, except for wings)

WINGS	Two mottled brown back feathers from ringneck pheasant, trimmed to shape (these feathers are located right at the root of the tail feathers); wings: 16mm long

Modern Fly
Dressings
for the
Practical
Angler
112

Mayfly nymphs. Left to right: *Hexagenia*,
Isonychia, *Stenonema*.

Hair-wing Hendrickson dun.

Cut-wing *Isonychia* dun.

Realistic Michigan mayfly.

Realistic March Brown (American).

Isonychia spinner.

Latex caddis larva.

Caddis pupae: latex on left, fur on right.

Hair-wing caddis adult.

Delta-wing caddis adult.

Latex stone fly nymphs: Large Western Salmon Fly nymph on left, Golden Stone Fly on right.

Letort Hopper (left) and Letort cricket.

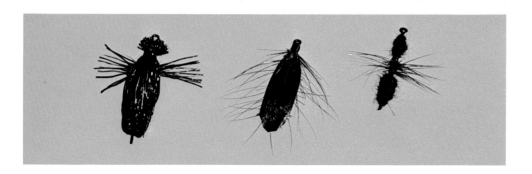

Deer-hair beetle, feather-wing beetle, and fur ant.

Hellgrammite larva.

REALISTIC DRESSING

BODY LENGTH	15mm
HOOK	Mustad #94842, Size 12
THREAD	Yellow, prewaxed 6/0
EXTENSION	Yellowish-tan spade hackle, or yellow breast feather from ringneck pheasant, with fibers reversed and set in silicone glue. (optional back markings made with a brown Pantone #154M); extension: 8mm long
TAILS	Two fibers from extension material; tails: 14mm long
WINGS	Same as cut-wing
THORAX	Fur dubbing (same as hair-wing body); thorax: 7mm long
HACKLE	Same as hair-wing
HEAD	Same as hair-wing

SPINNER DRESSING

HOOK	Mustad #94842, Size 10 to 12
THREAD	Yellow, prewaxed 6/0
WINGS	Lightest-gray deer body hair tips, tied spent; wings: 16mm long
TAILS	Wood duck flank feather fibers tied open V-shape or straight back; tails: 18mm long
BODY	Yellowish-brown fur dubbing
DUBBING FORMULA	2 parts medium brown, 1 part cream, and 1 part yellow

REMARK   This spinner is large enough to be dressed with the simplified extension and trimmed deer-hair thorax (see tying instructions).

TRADITIONAL DRESSING (AMERICAN MARCH BROWN)

HOOK	Mustad #94833, Size 10 to 12
THREAD	Orange, prewaxed 6/0
TAILS	Dark-ginger hackle fibers
WINGS	Well-marked wood duck flank feather
BODY	Light fawn-colored fox fur
HACKLE	Grizzly and dark ginger wound together
HEAD	Orange tying thread

MEDIUM BLUE-WINGED OLIVE

COMMON NAMES	Blue-Winged Olive, Small Dun Variant
GENUS	*Ephemerella*
SPECIES	*attenuata*

TIME OF APPEARANCE   Midmorning on Eastern streams, from late May through June

HAIR-WING DRESSING

HOOK	Mustad #94842, Size 16 to 18
THREAD	Olive, prewaxed 6/0
WINGS	Darkest-gray deer body hair tips (sometimes dyed dark gray); wings: 8mm long
TAILS	Golden badger hackle fibers; same length as wing

BODY	Yellowish-olive fur dubbing
HACKLE	Golden badger rooster neck hackle, tied parachute
HEAD	Olive tying thread
DUBBING FORMULA	2 parts medium olive, 1 part yellow, and 1 part gray beaver

CUT-WING DRESSING

(Same as hair-wing except for wings)

WINGS	Two blue-gray rooster body feathers trimmed to size; wings: 8mm long

REALISTIC DRESSING

BODY LENGTH	8mm
HOOK	Mustad #94842, Size 18
THREAD	Olive, prewaxed 6/0
EXTENSION	Small hen hackle or body feather dyed yellowish-olive, with fibers drawn reversed and set in silicone glue (a simplified extension-type may also be used instead); extension: 4mm long
TAILS	Three fibers from extension material; tails: 8mm long
WINGS	Same as cut-wing
THORAX	Fur dubbing (same as hair-wing body); thorax: 4mm long
HACKLE	Same as hair-wing
HEAD	Same as hair-wing

MEDIUM BLUE-WINGED OLIVE SPINNER

HOOK	Mustad #94842, Sizes 16 to 18
THREAD	Olive, prewaxed 6/0
WINGS	Palest-gray deer body hair tips, tied spent; wings: 8mm long
TAILS	Golden badger hackle fibers tied open V-shape, or three very stiff fibers tied straight back; tails: 10mm long
BODY	Dark olive-brown dubbing
HEAD	Olive tying thread
DUBBING FORMULA	2 parts dark brown and 1 part medium olive

TRADITIONAL DRESSING (BLUE-WINGED OLIVE)

HOOK	Mustad #94833, Size 16 to 18
THREAD	Olive, prewaxed 6/0
TAILS	Medium-blue-dun hackle fibers
WINGS	Two dark-blue-dun hackle tips
BODY	Yellowish-olive fur dubbing
HACKLE	Medium blue dun
DUBBING FORMULA	2 parts medium olive, 1 part yellow, and 1 part gray beaver

MICHIGAN MAYFLY DUN

COMMON NAMES	Michigan Caddis, Fish Fly, Grizzly Wulff

GENUS *Hexagenia*

SPECIES *limbata*

TIME OF APPEARANCE At twilight from mid-June through July, Midwest

HAIR-WING DRESSING

HOOK Mustad #94842, Size 10

THREAD Olive, prewaxed 6/0

EXTENSION Light-ginger spade hackle prepared as a simplified extension; extension: 20mm long

TAILS Two fibers from extension material; tails: 20mm long

WINGS Good amount of medium-gray deer body hair tips, set upright with center trimmed out for double-wing appearance; wings: 30mm long

THORAX Yellowish-tan fur dubbing; thorax: 10mm long

HACKLE One grizzly and one ginger wound together, parachute-style

HEAD Olive tying thread

DUBBING FORMULA 2 parts medium brown, 1 part yellow, and 1 part gray beaver

REALISTIC DRESSING

BODY LENGTH 30mm

HOOK Mustad #94842, Size 10

THREAD Olive, prewaxed 6/0

EXTENSION Wood duck flank feather with fibers reversed and set in silicone glue (if extension is too light when finished, tint it to a yellowish-tan with Pantone Marker; optional back markings are made with a purplish-brown Pantone #438M); extension: 20mm long

TAILS Two fibers from the extension material; tails: 22mm long

WINGS Two medium-blue-dun rooster body feathers trimmed to shape; wings: 30mm long

THORAX Fur dubbing (use hair-wing formula)

HACKLE Same as hair-wing

HEAD Same as hair-wing

MICHIGAN MAYFLY SPINNER

HOOK Mustad #94842, Size 10

THREAD Olive, prewaxed 6/0

EXTENSION Ginger-colored spade hackle prepared as simplified extension; extension: 20mm long

TAILS Two fibers from extension material; tails: 25mm long

WINGS Light-gray deer body hair tips, tied half-spent; wings: 30mm long

THORAX Butt ends and center one-third from wing material fashioned into deer hair body and trimmed to shape of thorax; portion in front

of wing filled in with fur
dubbing to match hair body

HEAD   Olive tying thread

TRADITIONAL DRESSING
(GRIZZLY WULFF—
AUTHOR'S CHOICE)

HOOK	Mustad #94833, Size 6
THREAD	Black, prewaxed 6/0
TAILS	Brown calf tail
WINGS	Brown calf tail
BODY	Pale-yellow floss, lacquered
HACKLE	Brown and grizzly, inter-wound
HEAD	Black

WHITE-WINGED EPHORON DUN

COMMON NAMES	White Fly, White Miller
GENUS	*Ephoron*
SPECIES	*leukon*

TIME OF APPEARANCE On some Eastern and Midwestern streams at twilight, during the months of August and September. The Potomac River in Maryland has blizzard hatches of the *Ephoron* genus the last two weeks of July, but of a species much larger than *leukon* and dressed on Size 8 to 10 hooks. I use the same dressing for both flies.

HAIR-WING DRESSING

HOOK	Mustad #94842, Size 14
THREAD	White, prewaxed 6/0
WINGS	White deer body hair tips; wings: 12mm long

TAILS	Pale-blue-dun hackle fibers; tails: 12mm long
BODY	White fur dubbing
HACKLE	Creamy-white rooster hackle, tied parachute
HEAD	White tying thread

CUT-WING DRESSING

(Same as hair-wing, except for wings)

WINGS	Two creamy-white rooster body feathers trimmed to shape; wings: 12mm long

REALISTIC DRESSING

BODY LENGTH	12mm
HOOK	Mustad #94842, Size 16
THREAD	White, prewaxed 6/0
EXTENSION	Small white spade hackle with fibers drawn reversed and set in silicone glue; extension: 6mm long
TAILS	Three fibers from extension material; tails: 12mm long
WINGS	Same as cut-wing
THORAX	White fur dubbing; thorax: 6mm long
HACKLE	Same as hair-wing
HEAD	Same as hair-wing

SPINNER DRESSING

HOOK	Mustad #94842, Size 14
THREAD	White, prewaxed 6/0
WINGS	White deer body hair tips, tied spent; wings: 12mm long

Modern Fly
Dressings
for the
Practical
Angler
116

TAILS   Palest-blue-dun hackle fibers tied open V-shape or straight back; tails: 16mm long

BODY   White fur dubbing

HEAD   White tying thread

TRADITIONAL DRESSING
(WHITE MILLER—AUTHOR'S CHOICE)

HOOK   Mustad #94833, Size 8 to 14

THREAD   White, prewaxed 6/0

TAILS   White hackle fibers

WINGS   White duck quill sections set upright

BODY   White fur dubbing

HACKLE   White rooster hackle

HEAD   White

6
Caddis Flies

Perhaps the most significant development in trout fishing within the past few years is an all-out study of caddis flies in their various stages of development. While imitations of the Trichoptera have been around for many years, they have always been treated as second-class citizens and used only in dire emergencies. But caddis flies are more common for longer periods of time than even the precious mayfly on most streams, and recently there have been a number of very significant literary contributions to the angler's library, written by distinguished American authors. Leonard M. Wright, Jr., is the author of a thinking man's guide to trout angling, *Fishing the Dry Fly as a Living Insect: An Unorthodox Method* (E. P. Dutton & Co., New York, 1972). Wright opens a whole new chapter in American dry-fly-fishing, teaching us how to fish the caddis flies. One of Ernest Schwiebert's contribu-

tions to the world of angling is his book *Nymphs; A Complete Guide to Naturals and Their Imitations* (Winchester Press, New York, 1973), in which he outlines the important Trichoptera larval and pupal stages through descriptions and magnificent drawings of each individual insect. Thanks to these two authors, the mystery of a caddis fly's behavior in its surface or subsurface environment is somewhat clearer in everybody's mind, not only to the angler whose joy it is to fool the fish with a fly on a delicate tippet, but to the fly-dresser as well, whose never-ending task it is to arrange his materials on the hook in an orderly manner so that the ultimate result will be an artificial that closely resembles the natural insect in size, form, and color.

In their underwater habitat the caddis flies differ from mayflies and stone flies in both appearance and development. After

119

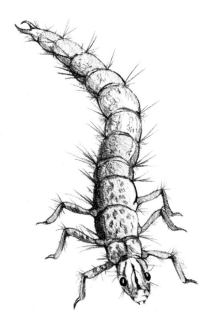

Caddis larva

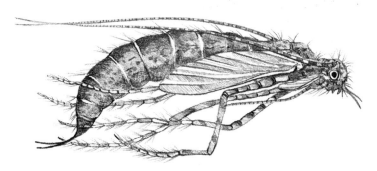

Caddis pupa

**Modern Fly
Dressings
for the
Practical
Angler
120**

Caddis adult

hatching from the egg they appear as wormlike larvae that, after completion of growth, change into a pupal stage and remain as such for a couple of weeks or longer, depending on the species, after which they rise to the surface and emerge as winged adults. Some caddis larvae are often referred to as caddis worms and move about freely without any visible protection, while others build a protective case of underwater fragments such as leaves, small sticks, and fine sand.

DRESSING THE CADDIS LARVA, STEP BY STEP

The little wormlike caddis larvae vary in size from 4mm to 16mm in length and have the appearance of a slim cylindrical worm with a dark-brownish thorax and a dirty-colored abdomen. They are found throughout America; many streams and ponds are blessed with a number of species that can provide good fishing all season long. To determine the size and color of the larvae in the area you are fishing, it is fairly simple to collect them. They are usually found on the rocky stream bottom and between stones in fairly shallow water.

The caddis larvae are not complicated to make, and the patterns I use are not given any entomological classification, but merely represent a long list of different species found in our fishing waters.

For many years I have used different kinds of fur for the abdomen of my caddis larvae and fished them with good results throughout the country. But nothing can beat latex for effectiveness and ease of dressing. Raleigh Boaze, Jr., of Brunswick, Md., discovered the use of latex as a super material for his "Ral's Caddis," a series of artificials that after a short while have become the center of attention in the angling world. What Raleigh didn't know was that he had opened a whole new chapter in American fly-dressing with his discovery, which once again proves that a fly-tyer never graduates. The series of caddis larva imitations in this book are those of the old design, but the abdomen portion now incorporates Raleigh's latex material tinted with Pantone Markers that are keyed to the color of each larva. All the patterns are dressed alike on a Mustad #3906 hook, which has a sproat bend that permits you to start the abdomen portion midway down the bend to incorporate a slight curve in the artificial. Since the normal habitat of the larva is at the bottom of the stream, they must be fished deep and will require additional weight, which is added by winding some .010 lead wire on the shank before the latex is wound on.

The larva I am using as a model for the dressing instructions is the celebrated Green Caddis Larva. Like so many other specimens I use as models, it was collected on the Beaverkill in the Catskills. The imitation is being dressed on a Mustad #3906 Size 10, which is about the average size.

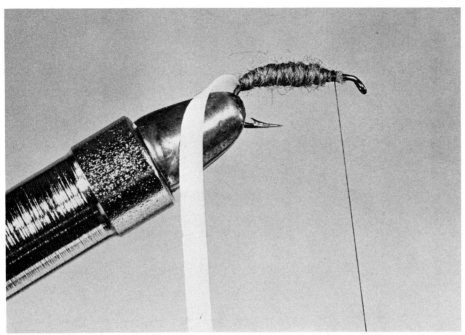

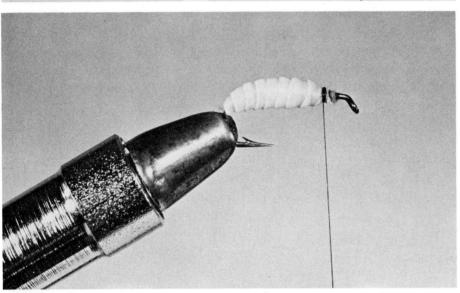

6-1 *Opposite.* Raleigh Boaze, Jr., shows me his method of winding latex for a pupa imitation. (Photo: Lefty Kreh) *Left.* This fat latex pupa has yarn over the windings of lead wire to add bulk. The finished imitation is tinted with a Pantone felt-tip pen (see discussion on page 139).

Caddis
Flies
123

GREEN CADDIS LARVA

HOOK	Mustad #3906, Size 8 to 18
THREAD	Brown, prewaxed 6/0
UNDERBODY	Tying thread and .010 lead wire
ABDOMEN	Natural latex strip, $^3/_{32}''$ wide, tinted
THORAX	Darkest-brown-dyed rabbit fur with guard hair mixed and spun in a loop
LEGS	Underside of thorax fur left long and picked out
HEAD	Brown tying thread
TINTING	Abdomen: green Pantone Marker #347M

1. Wind the entire hook shank with tying thread and tie in the tapered end of a latex strip midway down on the bend. Wind the .010 lead wire neatly with turns closely side by side on a portion of the shank as seen. Before you wind the latex the wire should be completely covered with tying thread to form a smooth, even underbody.

2. With very little stretch, wind the latex strip forward over the underbody in such a way that each turn overlaps the previous one by half its width. This produces the segmented effect that is characteristic of the natural larva. Secure the latex in front about a fourth of a body length from the eye with thread windings and cut the surplus latex.

Modern Fly
Dressings
for the
Practical
Angler
124

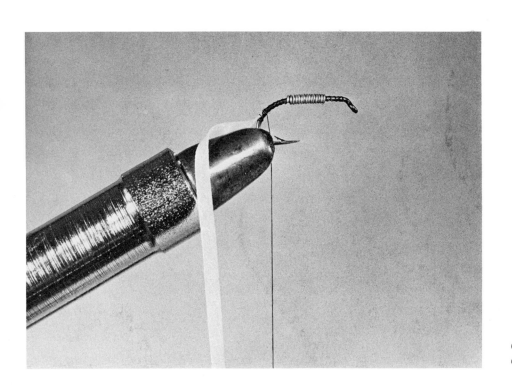

6-2 Dressing the Green
Caddis Larva, Step 1.

6-3 Step 2.

Caddis
Flies
125

6-4 Step 3.

6-5 Step 4.

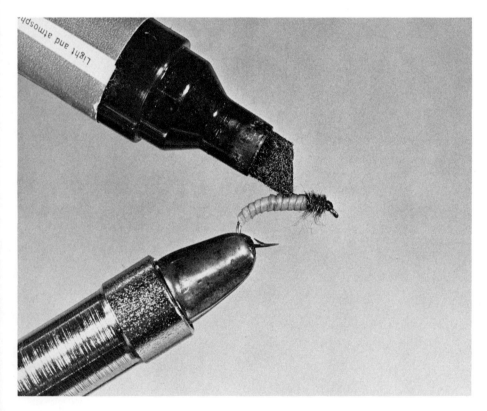

3. Form a 3-inch spinning loop and spin a small amount of the thorax fur into a dubbing.

4. Apply a small amount of clear cement on the shank and wind the dubbing on the thorax portion and tie off in front. Cut the surplus dubbing and trim the thorax on

126

6-6 The finished latex Green Caddis Larva.

top and both sides with your scissors. The underside is left long and picked out a little more to represent the legs. Add some clear cement on the head, which is wound of tying thread, and tint the abdomen portion with a Pantone Marker.

When the tinting is dry the larva is finished.

Additional Larva Dressings

WHITE CADDIS LARVA

HOOK	Mustad #3906, Size 8 to 18
THREAD	Brown, prewaxed 6/0
UNDERBODY	Tying thread and .010 lead wire
ABDOMEN	Natural latex strip, $^3/_{32}''$ wide
THORAX	Darkest-brown-dyed rabbit fur with guard hair mixed and spun in a loop
LEGS	Underside of thorax left long and picked out
HEAD	Brown tying thread
TINTING	None

OLIVE CADDIS LARVA

HOOK	Mustad #3906, Size 8 to 18
THREAD	Brown, prewaxed 6/0
UNDERBODY	Tying thread and .010 lead wire
ABDOMEN	Natural latex strip, $^3/_{32}''$ wide, tinted
THORAX	Darkest-brown-dyed rabbit fur with guard hair mixed and spun in a loop
LEGS	Underside of thorax left long and picked out
HEAD	Brown tying thread
TINTING	Abdomen: yellow-olive Pantone Marker #104M

GRAY CADDIS LARVA

HOOK	Mustad #3906, Size 8 to 18
THREAD	Brown, prewaxed 6/0
UNDERBODY	Tying thread and .010 lead wire
ABDOMEN	Natural latex strip, $^3/_{32}''$ wide, tinted
THORAX	Darkest-brown-dyed rabbit fur with guard hair mixed and spun in a loop
LEGS	Underside of thorax left long and picked out
HEAD	Brown tying thread
TINTING	Abdomen: gray Pantone Marker #413M

ORANGE CADDIS LARVA

HOOK	Mustad #3906, Size 8 to 18
THREAD	Brown, prewaxed 6/0
UNDERBODY	Tying thread and .010 lead wire
ABDOMEN	Natural latex strip $^3/_{32}''$ wide, tinted
THORAX	Darkest-brown rabbit fur with guard hair mixed and spun in a loop
LEGS	Underside of thorax fur left long and picked out
HEAD	Brown tying thread
TINTING	Abdomen: orange Pantone Marker #150M

YELLOW CADDIS LARVA

HOOK	Mustad #3906, Size 8 to 18
THREAD	Brown, prewaxed 6/0

Modern Fly
Dressings
for the
Practical
Angler
128

UNDERBODY	Tying thread and .010 lead wire
ABDOMEN	Natural latex strip $^3/_{32}''$ wide, tinted
THORAX	Darkest-brown-dyed rabbit fur with guard hair mixed and spun in a loop
LEGS	Underside of thorax fur left long and picked out
HEAD	Brown tying thread
TINTING	Abdomen: yellow Pantone Marker #115M

DRESSING THE CADDIS PUPA, STEP BY STEP

The most vulnerable time in a caddis fly's life is when it terminates the lease on its protective shelter built of sand, small stones, sticks, and other debris, in which it has remained enclosed for the duration of pupation. It must now swim to the surface and appear in its adult stage. During the final journey to the surface the fish are waiting, and, needless to say, many caddis pupae end their lives long before they reach their final destination and become a "fluttering adult."

Good imitations of the pupae are rare, and until recently no attempt had been made to bring them into order in the form of a series of artificials designed specifically to represent the many species of caddis found in America. Nevertheless, anglers successfully overcame the handicap by using traditional wet flies in the same general color and size as those of the migrating pupae with some success, which seems to prove my own theory that many of the wet flies designed by pioneering fly anglers were not meant to imitate a "drowned" mayfly, but rather inconspicuously imitated the pupae.

The length of the fully developed natural pupa ranges from 4mm to 30mm, depending on the species. The pupa's anatomy is much like the adult's, with the exception of the wings. The thorax and abdomen portion is developed distinctly, but the wings, which are contained in the wing cases located on each side of the thorax, are slanted down and project toward the rear, covering portions of the abdomen sides. On top of the head are two long antennae that appear to be fully developed, and the legs are clearly visible and slanted back past the posterior end of the abdomen. For the purpose of fishing, it would be a foolish and time-consuming job to make an imitative copy of each of the many hundreds of pupae in existence, so I have used Eric Leiser's "size and color" approach in designing my pupa imitations, which means that a few flies in several colors and many sizes will cover the needs for fishing anywhere in the country.

The biggest problem in imitating the naturals is to incorporate the glistering sheen of the silvery air bubbles trapped within the translucent pupal skin. When the seal was added to the list of endangered species there were a few moments of panic. Now there is Seal-Ex, a seal-fur substitute that is available from your material supplier. It is rich in sheen and translucency and lends itself magnificiently to the pupa dressings. Because of its coarseness, Seal-Ex can be mixed with some rabbit or mink fur of the same color for dressing the smaller sizes without sacrificing its effectiveness.

When fishing the pupa, one must try to imitate its natural movements and rise to the surface. This is best done by casting it upstream and letting it sink down before applying rhythmic movements with the rod tip and giving a swimming motion to the artificial as it works its way up. To hasten the sink rate, I often apply some windings of .010 lead wire on the hook shank before it is dressed.

For the tying instructions I have chosen a Dark Brown Caddis Pupa dressed on a Mustad #3906, Size 10. The Dark Brown is the representative for a number of important artificials that can be fished in both Eastern and Western streams. When dressed in different sizes they will match most of the dark-brown naturals found in the area being fished. If in doubt about which color pupa to use, I collect and open some caddis cases that are closed on both ends, which means that pupation is in progress, and thus determine the color and size found in a particular stream. Like the caddis larva, the pupa is fairly easy to dress, and I often use my streamside tying kit right on the spot if additional flies are needed.

Modern Fly
Dressings
for the
Practical
Angler
130

DARK BROWN CADDIS PUPA

REPRESENTING   Grannom (Size 10 to 14), Dark Blue Sedge (Size 10 to 14), Dark Brown Sedge (Size 6 to 8)

AVAILABILITY   The dark-brown variety of caddis pupa are found in both Eastern and Western streams, and I have had some very fine fishing particularly in Northeastern streams with both the Grannom and the Dark Blue Sedge. It seems that the fish will take this type of artificial more readily when some motion is generated to the fly with erratic movements of the rod tip. Even dragging it in the surface film has stirred up some violent strikes.

BODY LENGTH	9 to 17mm
HOOK	Mustad #3906, Size 6 to 14
THREAD	Brown, prewaxed 6/0
ABDOMEN	Dark-brown Seal-Ex dubbing, or latex dyed dark brown
WING CASES	Dark-gray duck quill sections
THORAX AND LEGS	Well-marked guard hairs and fur from the back of brown rabbit dyed dark brown
HEAD	Brown tying thread
DUBBING FORMULA	No mixing
TINTING	None

1. Attach the tying thread in front and wind it to a position midway down the hook bend. (If additional weight is de-

6-7 Dressing the Dark Brown
Caddis Pupa, Step 1.

sired, it should be added now by winding
some .010 lead wire on the shank and covering it with tying thread.) Now form a
3-inch spinning loop and insert a moder-
ate amount of dubbing.

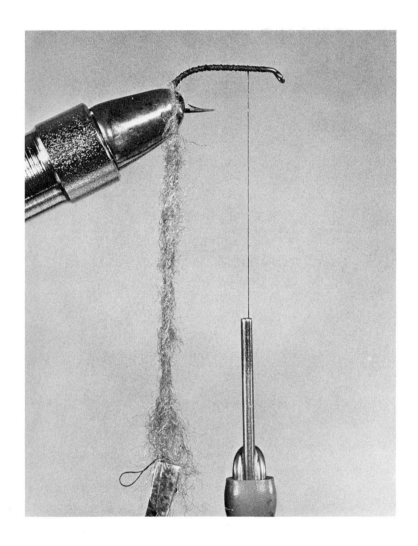

6-8 Step 2.

2. Using your heavy hackle pliers as a weight, spin a tapered "fur rope." It should be spun tightly enough to create a segmented effect when wound on, and be heavy enough to produce an abdomen of the proportion seen in the finished fly (see Fig. 6-15).

3. Apply a small amount of clear cement on the hook shank and wind the dubbing forward with close turns to a position one-fourth of a body length from the eye. Secure the dubbing tightly with tying thread at that point and trim away the surplus. Now trim the body portion lightly with your scissors, removing uneven spots and stray fibers.

6-9 Step 3.

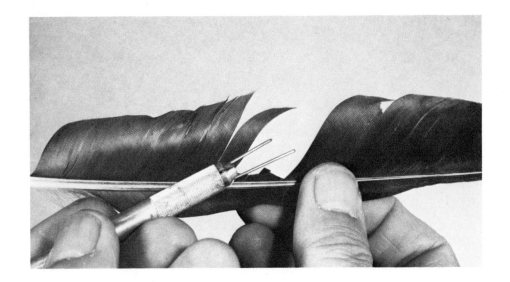

6-10 Step 4.

6-11 Step 5.

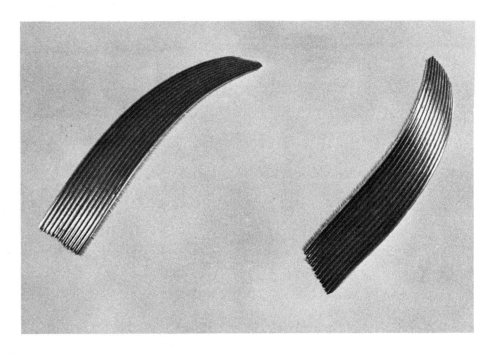

Modern Fly
Dressings
for the
Practical
Angler
134

4. Spray a left and a right duck wing quill with Krylon or other clear flexible adhesive, then cut a narrow segment from each feather. To make two wings of the same size, I use a homemade section divider consisting of an X-Acto knife handle with a trimmed paper clip held tightly in the jaws. The legs of the soft wire paper clip can be spread apart or brought closer together for the desired wing width.

5. Round the corners a little on each wing.

6. Tie in a wing section on each side in the position shown. It is important that the quill sections follow the contour of the front abdomen portion. This is best done by laying the wing section parallel with the body and slanting down a little. Holding it in that position, slowly take a complete turn of thread without applying pressure. Now form the quill section to the contour of the body and tighten the tying thread. They are tied in one at a time. Now form a 3-inch spinning loop at the wing.

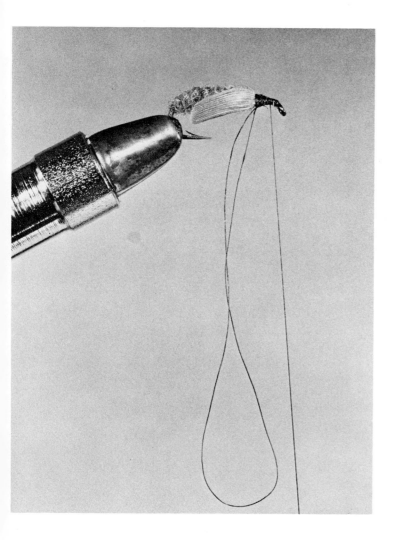

6-12 Step 6.

6-13 Step 7.

7. Cut the leg and thorax fur from the skin. It should be cut long enough so that the guard hairs will project beyond the hook bend a little when it is wound on. Insert the fur in the loop. Note the proportional placement; it is well spread out but still unblended as it came off the skin. With the loop thread as a guideline, it should be noted that the fur bunch is much longer to one side of the loop than to the other. In actuality, the longest portion has the fur and long guard hairs that will become the legs, and the short side becomes the thorax.

8. Spin a fur chenille using your heavy pliers as a weight, then hold it up above the hook and moisten it a little before stroking all the fur and guard hairs back so it appears to be coming out from one side of the loop only.

Modern Fly
Dressings
for the
Practical
Angler
136

6-14 Step 8.

Caddis
Flies
137

6-15 Step 9, the finished
Dark Brown Caddis Pupa.

**Modern Fly
Dressings
for the
Practical
Angler
138**

9. Apply a little clear cement on the hook shank, then wind the fur on in front of the abdomen and trim the top and sides a little, but leave the underside long to represent the legs. Wind a small head before applying the head cement and the pupa is finished. To make the pupa a little more durable, I often take a little sil- icone glue on my finger and smear it on top of the thorax, sides, and in front underneath. When applied very lightly it will not affect the performance of the artificial; in fact, it will make the guard hairs (legs) vibrate in a more confined area and look more natural when fished.

The Latex Pupa

While I use the latex body primarily for the caddis larva, it does make a very attractive abdomen for the larger pupa, although it lacks somewhat the fine translucency of Seal-Ex. The procedure has already been illustrated in Fig. 6-1.

First, tie in a strip of latex wide enough for the size pupa being dressed, in this case a size 10, for which the latex strip should be about ⅛ inch wide. When it is tied in midway down the bend of the hook, the additional weight should be applied if needed. To build up the body I use a fine strand of crewel wool of the same color as the finished abdomen. Be careful not to make the underbody too bulky; remember the latex will be wound over.

Then wind the latex strip forward over the underbody with very little stretch. It should be wound in such a way that each turn overlaps the previous one by half its width in order to get a nice segmented effect. Tie off the latex in front about one-fourth of a body length from the eye and cut the surplus.

The rest of the pupa is now finished in the same manner as described in the tying instructions for the dark brown caddis pupa. To get the color abdomen called for in the various dressings, the latex strips can either be dyed or tinted with Pantone marking pens.

Additional Pupa Dressings

Note: While all the dressings call for guard hair and fur from the back of a brown rabbit that has been dyed to give it a uniform color and darken the lighter guard hairs, this is not to say that other types of animals with the same characteristics cannot be used, or even be necessary, particularly in the smaller sizes. The Australian opossum is good for pupa dressings, as is the hare's mask. In any case, good judgment in selecting a substitute is needed to achieve the effect of the rabbit.

MEDIUM BROWN PUPA

REPRESENTING   Medium Brown Sedge (Size 8 to 10), Little Brown Sedge (Size 14 to 16)

AVAILABILITY   The Medium Brown Pupa is useful for fishing in Eastern and Western streams alike. For some reason I never fail to get a few fish on a Size 10 Medium Brown very early in the season. Since most streams are high and fairly fast at that time, I wind some .010 lead wire on the hook shank for extra weight before the body is applied.

BODY LENGTH   6 to 16mm

HOOK   Mustad #3906, Size 8 to 16

THREAD   Brown, prewaxed 6/0

ABDOMEN   Medium-brown Seal-Ex dubbing, or latex strip dyed medium brown

WING CASES   Medium-gray duck quill sections

THORAX AND LEGS	Well-marked guard hairs and fur from the back of a brown rabbit dyed brown
HEAD	Brown tying thread
DUBBING FORMULA	No mixing
TINTING	None

PALE BROWN PUPA

REPRESENTING	Spotted Sedge (Size 14), Speckled Sedge (Size 10)

AVAILABILITY Like most other caddis, the Pale Brown is found in both Eastern and Western rivers, and the artificials are effective most any time of the year, although late spring and early summer seem to be the time when they hatch. Try to fish it in the shallows late in the day or early evening by imitating the swimming movements so characteristic of the caddis pupa.

BODY LENGTH	9 to 13mm
HOOK	Mustad #3906, Size 10 to 14
THREAD	Brown, prewaxed 6/0
ABDOMEN	Pale-brown Seal-Ex dubbing, or latex strip dyed pale brown
WING CASES	Medium-gray duck quill sections
THORAX AND LEGS	Well-marked guard hairs and fur from the back of a brown rabbit dyed brown
HEAD	Brown tying thread
DUBBING FORMULA	3 parts buff and 1 part medium brown

TINTING The pale brown is not easy to dye, so if latex is used for the abdomen, it is better to tint it pale brown with a Pantone Marker #162M. The marker looks pink, but when applied generously it dries pale brown on latex.

GRAY CADDIS PUPA

REPRESENTING	Several gray and brownish-gray species

AVAILABILITY The Gray Pupa I carry in my fly box is a general representative of a number of caddis of that color, and I believe they will work anywhere in the country, although I have never found it to be as effective as the brown variety.

BODY LENGTH	6 to 13mm
HOOK	Mustad #3906, Size 10 to 16
THREAD	Brown, prewaxed 6/0
ABDOMEN	Grayish-brown Seal-Ex, or latex strip
WING CASES	Gray duck quill sections
THORAX AND LEGS	Well-marked guard hairs and fur from the back of a brown rabbit dyed brown
HEAD	Brown tying thread
DUBBING FORMULA	2 parts medium gray and 1 part medium brown
TINTING	If latex is used, it should be tinted with a light-gray Pantone Marker #413M

Modern Fly
Dressings
for the
Practical
Angler
140

CINNAMON SEDGE

REPRESENTING   Cinnamon Sedge

AVAILABILITY   My experience with the Cinnamon Pupa has been on Northeastern streams in late summer, but I see no reason why it should not be effective in other parts of the country.

BODY LENGTH   13 to 16mm

HOOK   Mustad #3906, Size 8 to 10

THREAD   Brown, prewaxed 6/0

ABDOMEN   Orangish-brown Seal-Ex dubbing, or latex strip

WING CASES   Dark-gray duck quill sections

THORAX AND LEGS   Well-marked guard hairs and fur from the back of a brown rabbit dyed dark brown

HEAD   Brown tying thread

DUBBING FORMULA   3 parts medium brown, 1 part burnt orange, and 1 part yellowish-orange

TINTING   If latex is used, it is first tinted with a yellowish-orange Pantone Marker #150M, then with a brown #154M; the brown should be dabbed on lightly

AMERICAN SAND SEDGE

REPRESENTING   Sand Sedge

AVAILABILITY   This pupa can be productive both in Eastern and Western streams and is active from late winter through early summer, depending on the location being fished.

BODY LENGTH   9 to 13mm

HOOK   Mustad #3906, Size 10 to 14

THREAD   Brown, prewaxed 6/0

ABDOMEN   Dirty-yellow Seal-Ex dubbing, or latex strip

WING CASES   Gray duck quill sections

THORAX AND LEGS   Well-marked guard hairs and fur from the back of a brown rabbit dyed brown

HEAD   Brown tying thread

DUBBING FORMULA   Add gray beaver to the yellow Seal-Ex until it appears as a dirty-yellow dubbing

TINTING   A latex abdomen should first be tinted yellow with a Pantone Marker #115M, then with a gray Pantone #413M; it is given a light touchup to produce the dirty-yellow appearance

BRIGHT GREEN PUPA

REPRESENTING   Western Caperer (Size 8 to 10), Dark Olive Sedge (Size 8 to 10)

AVAILABILITY   The subsurface stage of the Bright Green variety has been popular among serious fly-fishers for as long as I can remember, and whether you fish Eastern or Western streams, this is one pattern that should not be left out.

BODY LENGTH   13 to 16mm

HOOK   Mustad #3906, Size 8 to 10

THREAD   Brown, prewaxed 6/0

ABDOMEN   Bright-grass-green Seal-Ex dubbing touched up lightly on the back with black marking pen, or latex strip dyed bright green

WING CASES   Dark-gray duck quill sections

THORAX AND LEGS   Well-marked guard hairs and fur from the back of a brown rabbit dyed brown

HEAD   Brown tying thread

DUBBING FORMULA   No mixing

TINTING   The abdomen on pupae dressed with either Seal-Ex dubbing or latex should be touched up lightly on the back with a black marker; if this seems too dark, use a very dark green

PALE OLIVE PUPA

REPRESENTING   Olive Sedges

AVAILABILITY   Like the larger Bright Green Pupa, the Olives are favorites in the East and West both, where they represent a number of different species of caddis that are of importance to the angler.

BODY LENGTH   9 to 13mm

HOOK   Mustad #3906, Size 10 to 14

THREAD   Brown, prewaxed 6/0

ABDOMEN   Pale-olive Seal-Ex dubbing, or latex strip

WING CASES   Gray duck quill sections

THORAX AND LEGS   Well-marked guard hairs and fur from the back of a brown rabbit dyed brown

HEAD   Brown tying thread

DUBBING FORMULA   2 parts medium olive and 1 part yellow

TINTING   A latex abdomen should be tinted with a yellowish-olive Pantone Marker #104M

LARGE REDDISH-BROWN PUPA

REPRESENTING   Large Red Sedge

AVAILABILITY   The Reddish-Brown Pupa is among the largest of the caddis found in America and I believe it can be fished successfully anywhere in the country. Its large size should be particularly interesting for those who go after big fish at night.

BODY LENGTH   17 to 21mm

HOOK   Mustad #3906, Size 4 to 6

THREAD   Brown, prewaxed 6/0

ABDOMEN   Dark reddish-brown Seal-Ex dubbing, or latex strip dyed dark reddish-brown

WING CASES   Dark-gray duck wing quill sections

THORAX AND LEGS   Well-marked guard hairs and fur from the back of a brown rabbit dyed dark brown

HEAD   Brown tying thread

DUBBING FORMULA   2 parts dark brown and 1 part reddish-brown

TINTING   None

Caddis Pupae of Minute Sizes

There are times when the fish will start to feed on the tiniest members of the caddis family, some of them so small that it is impractical even to attempt to make a copy; it would appear as a mere speck. In later years, however, it has become fashionable to fish minute-sized artificials with midge rods and delicate 7X or 8X tippets. Most of the dressings of the larger pupae can be made up on smaller hook sizes such as 18, 20, and 22, with just a few changes in the material list. Narrow strips of latex are excellent for these tiny sizes, whereas the Seal-Ex dubbing must be substituted with a softer fur such as mink. The wing cases are completely omitted, but the thorax and leg method of dressing is retained, provided that some suitable guard-hair fur, such as hare's or Australian opossum mask, can be obtained. If this type of material is not on hand, they can be dressed by tying a few fibers under the body as a beard and a dark-brown fur thorax applied in front, using the same roll dubbing method as for a dry fly.

DRESSING THE CADDIS ADULT, STEP BY STEP

Except perhaps in some European countries, the caddis flies, or sedges as they are often called, have not been considered of major interest to the angler except in their subaquatic form. As a dry fly, their existence was somewhat overshadowed by flies of the major hatches. But a few years ago they suddenly accelerated in popularity and now demand equal space in our dry-fly boxes. Very often, I am sure, some of the traditional dries like the Light Cahill, Quill Gordon, and Adams have taken trout that somehow mistook them for being caddis flies, which doesn't make sense at all since trout are supposed to be selective and know the difference.

Of the patterns developed in recent years there are two types that have proved their worth. Both were designed by Larry Solomon of New York City, whose skill as an angler-writer is matched only by his innovative methods at the vise. Larry has spent a great deal of time in his research, studying the behavior pattern and availability of many of the most common caddis of interest to the angler. The first pattern is a hair-wing artificial; the wing consists of a bunch of deer body hair dressed as a down-wing, lying very low and parallel with the fur body. The tips of the wings extend beyond the hook bend and aid the fly in floating much like the tail on the traditional dry fly. The floating hackle is applied in the conventional dry-fly manner after the wing has been secured. Larry designed the hair-wing caddis to imitate the emerged adult and considers it as his standard caddis dry-fly imitation.

The second design is a delta-wing pattern; the deer-hair wing is replaced by hackle points tied on either side of the body in a jetlike manner. The specific intention of the delta-wing was to imitate a caddis that, for one reason or another, found itself in a disabled condition after emerging, unable to take off and an easy target for the trout, which will feed on such unfortunate insects in a very leisurely manner, completely contrary to their normal splashy approach. The availability of whole mink tails with very stiff guard hairs dyed in colors specifically for use in caddis fly dressing has made hair-wings a little easier to do, and in pace with changing times, I now use mink guard hairs for all my hair-wing dressings.

Adult caddis flies, or sedges, look very much like a moth and they are closely related. Their wings are rather long in relation to their relatively short body, and in comparison with the mayfly adult, seem completely out of proportion. When the insect is at rest the wings are folded and lie down over the body in the tentlike manner characteristic of most mothlike insects. The wings are rather hairy, a condition which undoubtedly prompted the entomologists to classify the caddis insects as Trichoptera (*trichos* = hair, and *pteron* = wing), which is coincidental to the fact that the artificial flies are called hair-winged caddis.

The two long antennae located on the forehead of the insect are omitted on the artificial as they have no bearing on effectiveness. Like most other insects, the caddis has six legs located on the thorax portion. The two rear legs are almost cov-

ered by the straddling wings when the caddis is at rest. The color of these insects varies according to species, and I suggest that you collect some specimens of the naturals on the stream being fished. During a heavy caddis hatch there may be several species of different colors intermixed. The trout are often selective, feeding only on one particular insect and ignoring the rest. Their peculiar behavior, dancing or fluttering about on or near the surface film, can be observed by kneeling down and focusing your attention on the water surface against the light. A small aquarium net is usually large enough to capture some specimens for closer examination.

The dressing procedure is quite simple, but until you have mastered the various manipulations, I suggest you use a Mustad #94833, 3X Super Fine Wire, Size 10. The color combination used for the instructions is incidental and may be changed to suit an individual taste.

HAIR-WING CADDIS

COMMON NAME	Hair-wing caddis with specific color named in front
ORDER	Trichoptera
GENUS AND SPECIES	Various
AVAILABILITY	Found on most streams and

lakes throughout the country from April through late September depending on the species. The heaviest concentration occurs in

Modern Fly
Dressings
for the
Practical
Angler
144

6-16 Dressing the hair-wing caddis adult, Step 1.

late afternoon and early evening and good days can often generate blizzardlike hatches.

HOOK Mustad #94833, Size 10 to 22

THREAD Brown, prewaxed 6/0

BODY Dark-olive fur dubbing

WINGS Medium-brown mink guard hairs, or hackle tips

HACKLE Medium-brown rooster hackle

HEAD Brown tying thread

1. Attach the tying thread in front and wrap the entire shank of the hook with thread to a position shown, then roll the fur dubbing on the tying thread.

Caddis Flies 145

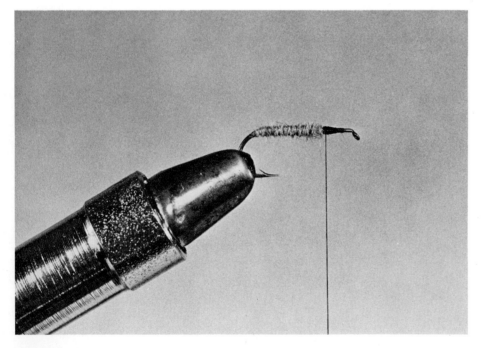

Modern Fly
Dressings
for the
Practical
Angler
146

2. Wind the dubbing on the hook shank in the same manner as for a traditional dry-fly body so that it covers two-thirds of the shank. Tie off the dubbing and cut the surplus, then wind some tying thread in front of the dubbed body, building up a level foundation for the wing, which will otherwise sit too high when tied in.

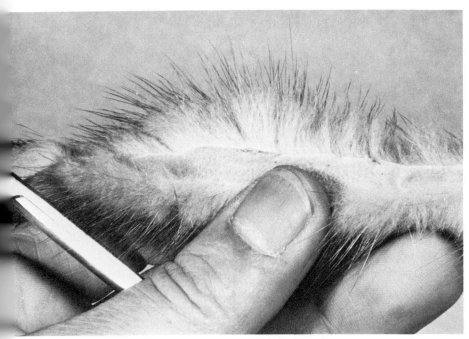

3. The mink tail guard hairs for the wing are best selected if the whole tail is cut up in thin strips. Insert a sharp knife in the underside of the hide and draw it with the direction of the hair for minimum waste.

Caddis Flies
147

6-19 Step 4.

Modern Fly
Dressings
for the
Practical
Angler
148

4. Cut a large bunch of hair close to the skin and remove the underfur. (Save the underfur, as it is the finest dry-fly dubbing you can obtain.) Align the hair in a lipstick tube, cartridge case, or small funnel. Insert the hair tips first, as seen. Shake the container and the hair aligns itself.

5. Place the hair on top of the hook with the tips extending a full body length beyond the hook bend. Take a couple of loose thread windings to hold them in place, then roll the hair down a little on each side of the shank and tighten them securely in that position. Trim the butt ends and apply a little clear cement. Make sure the wing is sitting flat and unflared.

Modern Fly
Dressings
for the
Practical
Angler
150

6. Tie in two dry-fly hackles selected properly for the hook size desired. They are tied in at the same time with the dull undersides together.

7. Wind the hackles one at a time in traditional dry-fly style and wind a small head in front before finishing the fly with a little clear cement on the thread windings.

6-22 Step 7, the finished hair-wing caddis adult imitation.

6-23 The delta-wing dressing for the caddis adult. The hackle-tip wings should be positioned as shown in the two views.

THE DELTA-WING DRESSING FOR THE CADDIS ADULT

The dressing procedures for this artificial are identical to that for the hair-wing, with the obvious exception of the wing.

Complete Steps 1 and 2 of the instructions for the hair-wing, then select two hackle tips of the proper color (in this case, medium brown) and tie them on in front on each side of the body so that they stand out at a 45-degree angle. The wings should be long enough to extend slightly beyond the hook bend. A properly set wing should be parallel with or slightly below the top of the body (see Fig. 6-23).

Attach and wind the hackles in the same manner as for the hair-wing, and the delta-wing caddis is finished (see Fig. 6-24).

6-24 The finished delta-wing caddis adult imitation, with hackles added.

6-25 Walt Dette's trimmed-hackle body for caddis imitations.

BODY AND HACKLE VARIATION

Modern Fly
Dressings
for the
Practical
Angler
154

An interesting method of body dressing and hackle trimming was shown to me by Walt Dette, the celebrated Catskill fly-dresser whose creations of fur and feather have set a standard for many a traditional fly pattern. He uses leftover hackle which he trims so that only the small stumps of barbules are left on the stem, then winds it on the hook shank with close turns laid side by side. This makes for a very translucent and extremely durable body and puts into use the less desirable hackles that always clutter the tying bench.

Dette's trimmed-hackle body ready for use with either a hair-wing or delta-wing

caddis is shown in Fig. 6-25. When Walt has finished his fly he likes it to sit very low on the water in a fashion characteristic of the natural insect, and here is where he breaks the unwritten rule of fly-tying. He trims the floating hackle. When reminded of his sin, he grins and makes reference to those artificials with no hackle at all. The hackle trimming is very specific and done with great care so that it will not ruin the balance or overall attractiveness of the fly. It is trimmed across underneath the body so the hackle fibers are of a length equal to the hook gap. This leaves the fibers on the side upon which the fly will float full length. A front view of Dette's trimmed floating hackle is shown in Fig. 6-26.

**Caddis
Flies
155**

Additional Caddis Dry-Fly Dressings

The dressings included in the list are those most commonly encountered on our trout streams, but the list is not all-inclusive, by any means. There are many hundreds of varieties for which new color combinations can be made up, and your time spent collecting specimens when on a fishing trip will pay dividends in the form of additional patterns. All the flies can be dressed either hair-wing or delta-wing style, or by substituting for the fur body a trimmed hackle of the same color and trimming the floating hackle as explained in the instructions; they can be dressed in the Dette style.

The size of the flies found in different parts of the country varies greatly; while the Eastern angler will tend to dress his flies in Size 14 to 22, the Westerner often needs larger flies for the big, fast rivers where even a Size 10 is too small. For summer steelheaders I carry the patterns dressed on Size 8 dry salmon hooks, and when the fish are taking on the surface they are deadly.

CADDIS DRY-FLY DRESSINGS

The dressings listed were compiled by Larry Solomon during the 1971, 1972, and 1973 seasons on the Beaverkill and Willowemoc in New York State. They are reprinted from *The Fly Tyer's Almanac 1975,* by permission of Crown Publishers, N.Y.

PERIOD OF EMERGENCE	BODY	WING	HACKLE	HOOK SIZE
Apr. to early May	Charcoal gray	Tannish gray	Light bronze dun	16
Early to mid May	Dark olive	Medium brown	Medium brown	16
Early to mid May	Light green	Tan	Light ginger	16
Mid to late May	Amber	Tannish gray	Medium brown	18
Mid to late May	Brown/gray	Brown/gray	Brown	18
Mid to late May	Grayish olive	Tan	Ginger	18
Late May*	Dark green	Brown/gray	Medium ginger	18
Late May to early June	Brown/gray	Tannish gray	Dark brown	16–18
Early June	Light olive	Tan	Ginger	18
Early June	Dark gray	Dark gray	Dark blue dun	20
Early June	Brown/gray	Brown/gray	Dark bronze/brown	16–18
Early June	Kelly green	Brown/gray	Bronze dun	22
Early to mid June	Grayish rusty cream	Charcoal gray	Light rusty dun	16
Early to mid June	Charcoal gray	Charcoal gray	Dark gray dun	14
Mid-June	Dark brown	Brown	Brown	16–18
Mid-June	Grayish olive	Tannish gray	Dark ginger	18
Mid-June	Brown/gray	Gray	Dark brown	20
Mid-June	Grayish olive	Tannish gray	Rusty dun	18
Early to mid Aug.	Pale olive	Light cream	Cream	22
Late Sept.	Dark green	Brown/gray	Brown	18

* This is one variety that was seen emerging on the surface. I'm sure there are others.

Caddis
Flies
157

7
Stone Fly Nymphs

The nymph of the adult stone fly is one of the most effective artificials I have ever used on a trout stream. Much like the pupa and larva of our caddis flies, they can be fished throughout the season anywhere in the country. I do not mean to imply that the species of a particular genus does not have a certain time of hatching, but their long growth period (as long as three years) makes them more available and they are ever present, crawling among rocks in the streambeds of swift rivers where sufficient oxygen can be generated for their existence. When they are ready to hatch they migrate to shallow areas and crawl up on rocks or debris; there their skin splits open and the adult insect appears. The hatching usually takes place very early in the morning. If you are walking along the rocky shores of a stream and you notice the empty skins on the stones it is an indication that a hatch is in

progress or has just taken place. At such times you can pick an artificial that closely matches the skins in size and color and often have some spectacular fishing, particularly if you get to the stream before daybreak.

The structural appearances of all stone fly nymphs are almost identical, so for the purpose of dressing the artificials they will be treated as such. The few minor differences that might be present from pattern to pattern will be explained in specific dressings.

Stone flies are generally flat throughout and have a long segmented abdomen with two tails at the posterior end. They are easily distinguished from other nymphs because they have two beautifully marked wing cases; the mayfly nymph has only one. They are located on the thorax portion, which represents the front half of the nymph. The head is quite large and flat

159

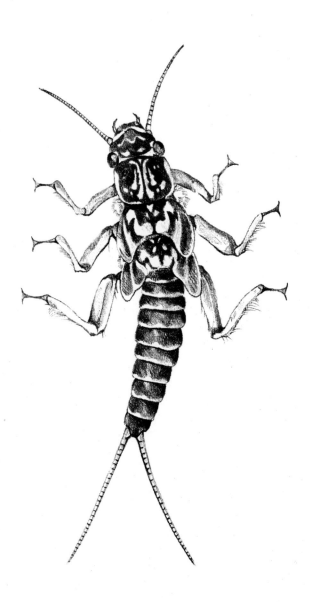

Stone fly nymph

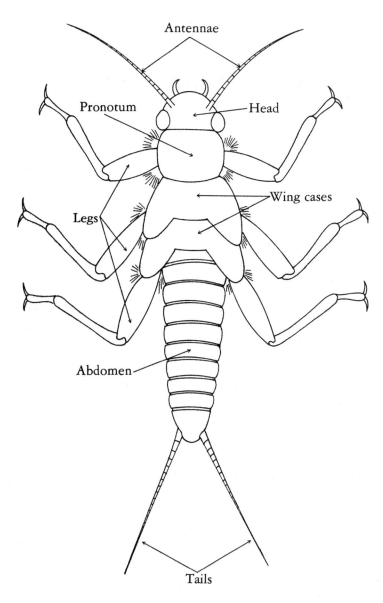

Anatomy of stone fly nymph

160

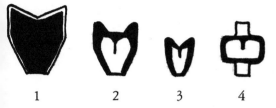

1   2   3   4

Wing cases vary a little from nymph to nymph. The three most practical forms and tinting procedures that I have come up with are shown in this drawing, along with a pronotum pattern (No. 4). There are no set rules on how to make and tint the wing case; you may have some better ideas. I use the forms here as follows: No. 1, Western Salmon Fly Nymph, Large Black Stone Fly; No. 2, Perla Stone Fly Creeper, Golden Stone Fly Nymph, Brown Stone Fly Nymph; No. 3, Reddish Brown Stone Fly Nymph, Early Black Stone Fly, Little Yellow Stone Fly, Little Green Stone Fly; No. 4, the pronotum, shown here as appropriate for using case No. 2 (it should always be tinted to coincide with the wing cases).

with two antennae that are about half as long as the tails. The six legs are rather strong in appearance and have a small claw on the end, which makes them ideally suited for a nymph that lives among rocks and debris on the stream bottom. The body of a mature nymph, excluding tails and antennae, is about 6mm to 50mm ($1/4$ inch to 2 inches) and ranges in color from pale yellow, amber, and tan to brown and black. In most cases the bottom portion of the nymph is much lighter than the top, if not entirely different. Those who care to collect some specimens for use as models will find that the empty skins found along the stream will do nicely, but they are pretty fragile. Live insects can be collected from the streambed by placing a large piece of screening or net downstream from the place you are searching, then roughing up the stream bottom and turning over stones and debris. The dislodged insects are carried into the collecting net by the current, after which they can be picked up and placed in suitable containers.

DRESSING THE STONE FLY NYMPH, STEP BY STEP

The nymph I am using as a model for the dressing instructions is a well-known Eastern species: *Perla capitata,* better known as the *Perla* Stone Fly Creeper in the East. The specimen I am copying was collected on the Beaverkill in the Catskills in the month of August, where the rocks in the shallows of Schoolhouse Pool were cluttered with nymphal shucks, and adult stone flies appeared everywhere along the banks in the early morning hours. Although the nymph can be fished throughout the season, my notes indicate that I have taken more fish on this particular artificial during the summer months. Unlike some of the large Western stone flies, *Perla* is rarely of any value in its adult stage dressed as a dry fly, and I don't carry any in my fly box.

The first and foremost consideration before starting to copy any specific insect is to evaluate its dimensions, and this is perhaps more important for stone flies than for any other insects because of their unique structure. Aside from having two distinct wing cases, there is one more important factor that makes them different from other nymphs and larvae: they have a smooth outer shell without hairy filaments, as opposed to the mayfly nymph with its breathing gills along either side of the abdomen. When dressing stone flies, I strongly urge that you closely follow the proportions prescribed and shown in the drawing, or the end result, regardless of your fly-tying skill, will be an absolute disaster.

PERLA STONE FLY CREEPER

BODY LENGTH   15 to 28mm

HOOK   Mustad #38941 3X Long, Size 4 to 10

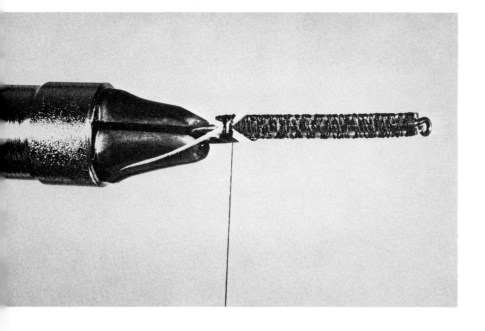

7-1 Dressing the Perla Stone Fly Creeper Nymph, Step 1.

THREAD	Yellow, prewaxed 6/0
UNDERBODY	Lead wire secured on either side of the hook shank
TAILS	Two white quill fibers tinted amber, half a body length
BODY	Natural latex strip, $^3/_{32}''$ to $^3/_{16}''$ and 6'' long, wound entire body length and tinted amber with brown back markings
WING CASES	Two pieces of natural latex trimmed to shape and tinted amber with brown markings
LEGS	Well-marked guard hair and back fur from a brown rabbit dyed amber
ANTENNAE	Two white quill fibers tinted amber, half a tail length
HEAD	Tying thread tinted brown on top and amber on bottom

TINTING The body, wing cases, tails, and feelers are tinted amber with a Pantone Marker #136M, which is a yellowish-orange color. After tinting the body once, in one direction only, from front to rear, give the top of the abdomen an extra coating, this time from rear to front, which will bring out the segmented effect. Now apply the back markings, using a brown Pantone Marker #154. First draw a line on each side of the abdomen, from the middle of the body down to the extreme posterior end, then draw one in the same direction down the middle of the top portion of the abdomen. This line should be narrow enough so the amber shows on each side. The wing-case markings are done with the same brown Pantone, in the pattern shown in the diagram.

1. Cover the entire hook shank with tying thread, from the eye to a point above the barb, then fasten a piece of .035 lead wire on each side of the shank. This is best done by fastening one at a time. When they are both tied on securely, straighten them up even along the shank with needlenose pliers. Now tie in the two tails and give the entire underbody a good coat of cement.

Stone Fly Nymphs 163

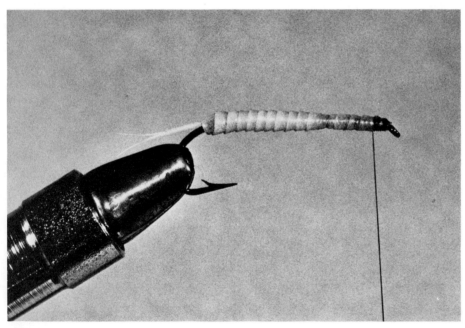

Modern Fly
Dressings
for the
Practical
Angler
164

2. Taper the end on a strip of latex $3/32''$ wide and about $6''$ long. Attach the latex on top of the underbody above the barb without creating a lump, then wind it forward over the underbody, making sure that each new wrap overlaps the previous one by half its width. Put only a little bit of stretch on the latex when you wind it. When you are a little past the middle of the body, the segmented abdomen portion is finished; the front thorax portion is best covered with the latex under heavy stretch with windings laid at random until the front is reached. Tie it off just short of the

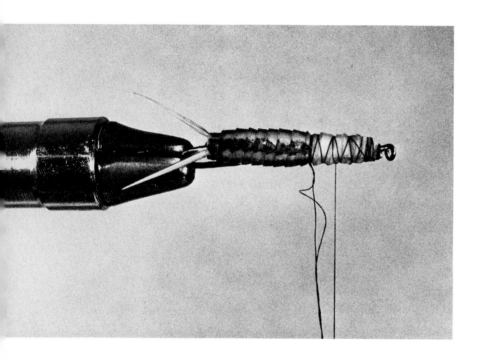

beginning of the underbody, fastening it securely with tying thread and a half-hitch before cutting the surplus.

3. Tint the tails and the entire body with the amber Pantone Marker and apply the back markings as diagrammed for the *Perla* nymph in the drawing. Now wind your tying thread back to approximately $1/8''$ before the middle of the body and form a 3-inch spinning loop.

Stone Fly Nymphs 165

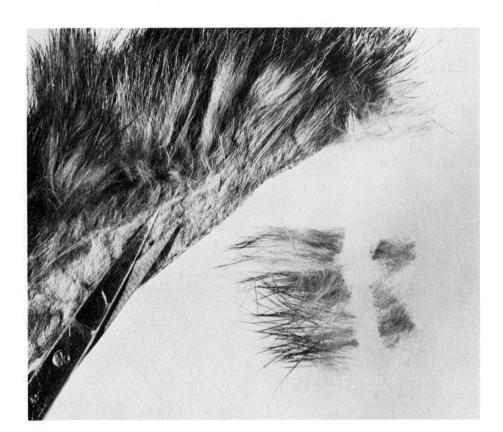

Modern Fly
Dressings
for the
Practical
Angler
166

4. Cut a bunch of fur and guard hair from the back of a brown rabbit skin dyed amber. The guard hairs should be well marked with dark brown. The whole bunch should be as long as half a body length.

7-5 Step 5.

5. Insert the fur in the loop. Note the proportional placement. It is well spread out, and the fur bunch is much longer to one side of the loop than to the other. The longest side has the fur and guard hair that will become the legs, and the short side becomes a padding for the wing case. Then spin the leg fur.

Stone Fly
Nymphs
167

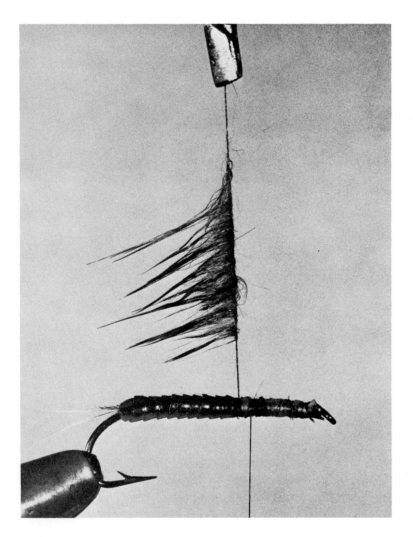

7-6 Step 6.

Modern Fly
Dressings
for the
Practical
Angler
168

6. Pull all the leg fur back and apply two
or three complete windings. Trim the top
fur away and leave the sides and bottom
long for the legs.

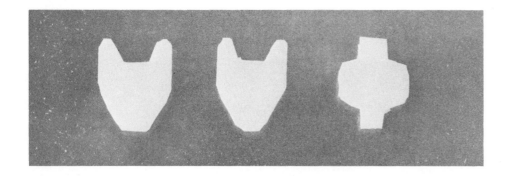

7-7   Step 7.

7-8   Step 8.

Modern Fly
Dressings
for the
Practical
Angler
170

7. Trim the two wing cases to shape with your scissors. The dimensions of the latex pieces from which they are cut should be 1½ times the width of the abdomen by 2 times the width of the abdomen. (Fig. 7-7 shows the wing cases and also the pronotum, an optional refinement discussed later.)

8. Tie in the first wing case with three or four turns of thread directly in front of the fur legs, then form another 3-inch spinning loop.

9. Before applying the second set of fur legs, the entire wing case is tinted amber. You will notice that the tinting will make it fall into place. When it has dried for a few seconds, the brown lines and markings are put on.

**Stone Fly
Nymphs
171**

7-10 Step 10.

Modern Fly
Dressings
for the
Practical
Angler
172

10. Spin the second set of fur legs as you did the first and wind them on in front of the wing. Tie in the second wing case as you did the first one and tint it in the same manner. Cut the surplus latex and wind over the ends at the head. When the underbody and latex is completely covered in front, tie in the antennae in widespread fashion.

11. Cut the surplus ends of the antenna material and wind a neat head before fin-

7-11 Step 11, the finished
Perla Stone Fly Creeper
Nymph.

ishing off with a whip finish. Tint the head and antennae amber on top and bottom, then make a thin brown line across the top between the wing case and the head, and one in front on top of the head between the antennae. Apply some head cement and the *Perla* stone fly creeper is finished. The underside of the nymph can be left as it is or trimmed away in the middle under the thorax, leaving the sides to represent the legs.

7-12 The pronotum, which is optional, is tied in ahead of the front wing. Read the instructions carefully to see how to incorporate this refinement.

Modern Fly
Dressings
for the
Practical
Angler
174

The basic principles of the preceding tying instructions are used for all the stone fly nymph patterns with latex body and wing cases. Careful judgment of the underbody needed for a particular pattern is of utmost importance; while my instructions above call for lead wire as a means of creating a firm, flat surface on which the latex can be wound, lead is by no means the only possible material. I often use monofilament of the appropriate thickness; it alters the sink rate of the artificial when it is needed for shallow fishing.

When designing the latex stone fly nymph, I deliberately left out a segment on top of the thorax that in the natural is called the pronotum. The part is located between the front wing case and the head. For the purpose of fishing it doesn't matter whether it is there or not, at least not to us common folks, but for the benefit of perfectionists who insist that it must be there, I will briefly explain how it can be added. At Step 3 in the tying instructions, instead of winding the tying thread back to 1/8″ before the middle is reached, it is

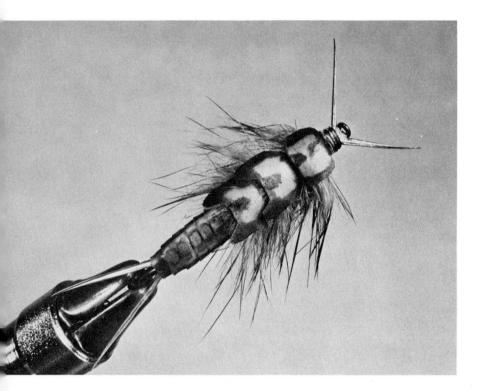

7-13 The finished Perla Stone
Fly Creeper Nymph with
pronotum.

wound exactly to the middle, where the first spinning loop is made. The following steps are then performed exactly as given until you get to Step 9. When the wing case is secured as explained in that step, the additional latex piece that will form the pronotum must be tied in. It is trimmed to shape from material of the same width as the wing cases, as seen in Fig. 7-7. Tie in the latex piece on top of the thorax directly in front of the wing case with thread windings that will fall exactly over those that secured the wing case, then form a 3-inch spinning loop for the additional leg fur (see Fig. 7-12). Wind on the legs, trim away the top fur, and fold the latex forward over the leg section. Trim the latex to the length needed, taper the end, and tie it down in front. The head and antennae are now completed as previously described. The pronotum section is now tinted with amber, and the brown markings are applied. One finished *Perla* Stone Fly Creeper with pronotum is shown in Fig. 7-13.

SELECTED STONE FLY
NYMPH DRESSINGS

Note: Since most of the nymphs included in this list of patterns can be dressed in different sizes, the wire diameter needed for the flat underbody is not specified; it must be chosen by the tyer to arrive at the body proportions mentioned earlier in this chapter and shown in the drawing. Some of the smallest nymphs are dressed without an underbody or with just a single piece of thin wire attached on one side of the hook shank only. It is not practical to use lead wire with a diameter larger than .035, so the underbody for the largest nymphs, where flatness is more evident, must have added width. This is accomplished by winding a couple of layers of light-colored floss on the hook shank before the lead wire is attached on the sides. To even further enlarge the underbody, it is wound with several layers of the same color floss after the lead wire is secured. It is important to saturate such a structure with clear cement and let it dry before the latex is wound on. The latex strips for the body are usually cut in three widths— $^3/_{32}''$, $^1/_8''$, and $^3/_{16}''$—but can of course be cut to suit your needs.

Modern Fly
Dressings
for the
Practical
Angler
176

LARGE WESTERN SALMON
FLY NYMPH

GENUS *Pteronarcys*

SPECIES *californica*

AVAILABILITY Found all season in large Western rivers. The hatching time depends to some degree on the area being fished, but it usually starts at the end of April in the westernmost rivers and gradually occurs later as you move eastward.

The realistic appearance of the large latex nymphs has made them extremely effective. I rarely dress them any larger than Size 4, which enables me to cast even a heavily weighted nymph quite a distance with an 8-foot rod.

BODY LENGTH	15 to 37mm
HOOK	Mustad #38941 3X Long, Sizes 2 to 10
THREAD	Brown, prewaxed 6/0
UNDERBODY	Lead wire secured on either side of the hook shank
TAILS	Dark-brown wing quill fibers, one-fourth body length
BODY	Latex strip dyed medium brown and wound over underbody
WING CASES	Two pieces of latex dyed medium brown and trimmed to shape
LEGS	Well-marked guard hairs with fur from the back of a brown rabbit dyed medium brown
ANTENNAE	Two dark-brown wing quill fibers, same length as tails
HEAD	Tying thread tinted
TINTING	Before tying in the legs and

wing cases, the entire body is tinted with a yellowish-orange Pantone Marker #150M. This is done to give the finished nymph an orange-brown cast. The body is now tinted dark brown with Pantone #464M on the *top and sides only*. This is not a solid tinting, but

7-14 The Large Western
Salmon Fly Nymph.

should be done in a manner that will show some of the orange-brown base color down the middle of the back. The bottom is left as is: orange-brown. The wing cases are treated in the same manner. First tint them yellowish-orange, and then with a dark-brown Pantone. This is a solid tinting, but a good effect is obtained by leaving a thin rim of the base color showing at the edges all around and as a separation between the front wing case and the head. When the antennae are tied in, the head is formed with tying thread, then tinted brown on top and yellowish-orange on the bottom before clear cement is applied. The tails and antennae can be taken from a white goose wing feather (fibers on the narrow leading edge) and tinted brown with Pantone instead of using a dyed feather. This assures the same coloration as the rest of the body.

LARGE BLACK STONE FLY NYMPH

GENUS   *Pteronarcys*

SPECIES   *dorsata*

AVAILABILITY   This species is found in both Eastern and Western rivers and is the largest and most impressive stone fly in the country. Like some of the other large nymphs, it is best fished in the early morning hours when the naturals migrate to the shallow areas and hatch. According to anglers who have followed *dorsata* activities, the hatching period starts in May and lasts well into the summer months.

Dressing the *Pteronarcys dorsata* imitation is much like the *P. californica* imitation with the exception of color.

BODY LENGTH   15 to 50mm

HOOK   Mustad #79580 4X Long, Size 1 and 2
Mustad #38941 3X Long, Size 2 to 8

THREAD   Brown, prewaxed 6/0

UNDERBODY   Lead wire secured on either side of the shank

TAILS   Darkest-gray goose quill fibers tinted brown, one-fourth body length

BODY   Latex strip dyed gray and wound over underbody

WING CASES   Two pieces of latex dyed gray and trimmed to shape

LEGS   Well-marked guard hairs with fur from the back of a brown rabbit dyed darkest brown

ANTENNAE   Darkest-gray goose quill fibers tinted brown, same length as tails

HEAD   Brown tying thread

TINTING   Because the color of the natural varies from stream to stream, it is often helpful to secure a sample from the area you are fishing and select your material and tinting color accordingly. The basic nymph I use is dressed with the material mentioned above, and I first tint the entire body brown with a Pantone Marker #464, top and bottom. The top and sides are then tinted with a dark-gray Pantone #404M. Unlike the *californica* species, the *dorsata* imitation is tinted solid dark gray, using lengthwise strokes with the marker back and forth to bring out a distinct segmented effect. The wing cases are tinted brown first, then a solid dark gray, leaving a rim of the base color showing at the edges as with the *californica* imitation. The tails and antennae on this nymph can be left natural if they are dark enough; otherwise they should be tinted brown as indicated above the dressing. This tinting method produces a very realistic slate-brown-looking nymph with a lighter belly.

GOLDEN STONE FLY NYMPH

GENUS   *Acroneuria*

SPECIES   *californica*

AVAILABILITY   Like *Pteronarcys dorsata* and *P. californica*, this large, handsome stone fly is found in the fast Western rivers, where it can grow to a length of over 40mm, although artificials are rarely dressed larger than a Size 2 3X Long, or approximately 35mm. The hatching takes place in June and July, depending on locale, and many anglers consider this fly one of the most important to have for Western fishing. This nymph is dressed exactly like the *Perla* Stone Fly Creeper (*Perla capitata*) used

Modern Fly
Dressings
for the
Practical
Angler
178

for tying instructions earlier in the chapter; the materials and tinting method are identical. However, since it is often dressed larger than the *Perla*, I use Mustad hooks #38941 3X Long, Size 2 to 8.

BROWN STONE FLY NYMPH

GENUS   *Acroneuria*

SPECIES   Representative of several medium-size nymphs of the genus

AVAILABILITY   Various representatives of this nymph can be fished successfully throughout the season in both Eastern and Western mountain streams. There is rarely any need for many sizes of this medium-size nymph and I carry only one, dressed on a Size 6 3X Long hook. I do, however, vary the color from medium and dark brown to blackish-brown.

BODY LENGTH	Approximately 25mm
HOOK	Mustad #38941 3X Long, Size 6
THREAD	Brown, prewaxed 6/0
UNDERBODY	Lead wire secured on either side of the hook shank
TAILS	Brown wing quill fibers
BODY	Natural latex strip wound over underbody
WING CASES	Two pieces of natural latex trimmed to shape
LEGS	Well-marked guard hairs with fur from the back of a light-brown rabbit dyed tan
ANTENNAE	Brown wing quill fibers
HEAD	Brown tying thread

TINTING   Tint the entire body portion with yellowish-orange Pantone #150, then tint the top and sides of the abdomen portion with a brown Pantone #464M. This can be tinted solid, or if you want to spend the time, try to tint each segment with brown so a little of the base body color is seen to imitate the ringed effect. The wing cases are tinted yellowish-orange first, then decorated heavily with brown in the same manner as for the *Perla capitata* imitation. For darker dressings I use the same basic material, but do the tinting with darker-brown and gray Pantone Markers.

EARLY REDDISH-BROWN STONE FLY NYMPH

GENUS   *Taeniopteryx*

SPECIES   Representative of the genus

AVAILABILITY   These small reddish-brown stone fly nymphs are very important to the Eastern angler who doesn't mind cold weather and icy line guides, and can provide good fishing from shortly after New Year's to early spring. The Western angler may find a species of *Taeniopteryx* in some mountain streams, but they arrive somewhat later than the Eastern variety. I should like to mention that this is one of the small stone fly nymphs that I keep as a backup for fishing all season if everything else fails.

BODY LENGTH	12 to 16mm
HOOK	Mustad #38941 3X Long, Size 10 to 12
THREAD	Brown, prewaxed 6/0
UNDERBODY	One very thin strip of lead wire on one side of the hook shank

TAILS	Brown cock pheasant center tail fibers
BODY	Latex strip $^3/_{32}''$ wide, dyed medium brown and wound over underbody
WING CASES	Two pieces of latex dyed medium brown and trimmed to shape
LEGS	Guard hairs with fur from the mask of an Australian opossum dyed brown
ANTENNAE	Brown cock pheasant center tail fibers
HEAD	Brown tying thread

TINTING   The top and sides are tinted with a reddish-brown Pantone Marker #499M, leaving the bottom medium brown. It should be tinted solidly but lightly, taking at least one stroke from rear to front, which brings out the segmented effect. The wing cases are marked as outlined earlier in the drawing. The tails and antennae should be tinted lightly with reddish-brown marker, but the head need only be given a couple of applications of clear cement.

EARLY BLACK STONE FLY NYMPH

GENUS	*Capnia*
SPECIES	Representative of the genus
AVAILABILITY	These early black stone flies are found in both Eastern and Western rivers. The body of the nymph is very slender, and the smaller sizes can be well imitated by winding the latex strip directly on the hook shank without the lead strip on the side. I

usually add a very thin strip on the larger sizes, which are about 15 to 20mm long and dressed on Size 8 3X Long hooks. This nymph is on the move even earlier than the *Taeniopteryx*, so the angler can use it for late-winter fishing.

BODY LENGTH	10 to 20mm
HOOK	Mustad #38941, Size 8 to 14
THREAD	Black, prewaxed 6/0
UNDERBODY	One thin strip of lead wire secured on one side of the hook shank
TAILS	Thin dark-gray goose quill fibers
BODY	Latex strip $^3/_{32}''$ wide, dyed dark gray
WING CASES	Two pieces of latex dyed dark gray and trimmed to shape
LEGS	Dark-gray guard hairs with fur from the mask of an Australian opossum
ANTENNAE	Thin dark-gray goose quill fibers
HEAD	Black tying thread

TINTING   If good dark-gray color has been obtained by dyeing the latex, the body needs no tinting. It can be darkened, if necessary, with a gray Pantone Marker #404M. Wing-case markings are applied with the same gray marker in the pattern shown earlier in the drawing. These markings should appear almost black when finished.

LITTLE YELLOW STONE
FLY NYMPH

GENUS *Isoperla*

SPECIES Representative for the yellow nymphs of the genus

AVAILABILITY These flies are found in Eastern and Western rivers all summer long. I have observed heavy concentrations on the Beaverkill in the Catskills from July to September. Hal Mattes of Brooklyn, New York, a student and keen observer of the happenings on the stream, soon discovered that what at a distance appeared to be yellow mayflies were indeed small yellow stone fly adults. A Size 14 dry caddis fly imitation with yellow body, pale-dun hair wing, and yellow hackle took many fish, as did the little nymph fished in the shallow areas. The heaviest hatching activities come in late afternoon and early evening on both Eastern and Western streams.

BODY LENGTH	12 to 15mm
HOOK	Mustad #38941 3X Long, Size 10 to 12
THREAD	Pale yellow, prewaxed 6/0
UNDERBODY	None, or one very thin strip of lead wire on one side of the hook shank
TAILS	White goose quill fibers tinted yellow
BODY	Natural latex strip $^3/_{32}''$ wide
WING CASES	Two pieces of natural latex trimmed to shape
LEGS	Pale creamish-yellow belly fur with guard hairs from an Australian opossum
ANTENNAE	White goose quill fibers tinted yellow
HEAD	Pale-yellow tying thread
TINTING	The entire body, tails, and antennae are tinted with a yellow Pantone Marker #115M. Wing-case markings are made with a pale-olive-green Pantone Marker #104M.

LITTLE GREEN STONE
FLY NYMPH

GENUS *Alloperla*

SPECIES Representative of the genus

AVAILABILITY Like *Isoperla*, this nymph is found in both Eastern and Western streams, and is particularly useful for fishing during the summer months.

BODY LENGTH	11 to 16mm
HOOK	Mustad #38941 3X Long, Size 10 to 14
THREAD	Yellow, prewaxed 6/0
UNDERBODY	Thin strip of lead wire on one side of the shank
TAILS	White goose quill fibers tinted yellowish-green
BODY	Natural latex strip $^3/_{32}''$ wide
WING CASES	Two pieces of natural latex trimmed to shape
LEGS	Dyed pale-yellowish-green belly fur with guard hairs from an Australian opossum
ANTENNAE	White goose quill fibers tinted yellowish-green
HEAD	Yellow tying thread

TINTING The entire body, tails, antennae, and wing cases are tinted with a yellowish-green Pantone Marker #104M. Wing-case markings are applied with a pale-green Pantone #351M. The head is tinted with yellowish-green before the clear cement is added.

**Modern Fly
Dressings
for the
Practical
Angler
182**

8
Terrestrial Insects

As far as I can determine, there is little doubt that terrestrial fishing emanated on the Pennsylvania limestone streams near Carlisle, where Vince Marinaro and Charles K. Fox, two of America's most distinguished anglers, refined to a science the methods of angling with hoppers, crickets, beetles, and ants, aided by their tobacco-chewing friend Ross Trimmer, whose ability with rod and vise was overshadowed only by his ability to talk louder and laugh harder than anyone else. By sharing their experiences they laid the foundation of a new era of dry-fly fishing, which has been built upon enthusiastically by others. We are grateful to them not only for the opportunity of an extended dry-fly season, but also for giving the fly-tyer an excuse to work overtime at the vise.

BEETLES (COLEOPTERA)

On some trout streams, and it doesn't much matter where in the country, there is no artificial fly that works better than a small beetle, particularly a black one. On windy days they are often blown into the water and find themselves struggling on the surface for survival, but few manage to reach shore before falling prey to a hungry trout.

My favorite is one made from deer body hair that has been dyed black, although there are times when one dressed with natural dun-gray works well. I once met a delightful fellow on the stream who tied all his deer-hair beetles in white and carried waterproof marking pens of various colors in his vest so that he could always "match the beetle hatch"

8-1 Dressing the deer-hair
Black Beetle, Step 1.

no matter where he happened to be. While the deer-hair beetle is made entirely from one bunch of hair manipulated onto the hook in the form of the natural insect, there is a feather beetle which is more delicate and less bulky, a reason I suspect for choosing it when fishing over native browns in Pennsylvania's slow-moving limestone streams. I am including dressings for both types of beetles, two favorites of mine—though there are undoubtedly others that would work just as well.

Modern Fly
Dressings
for the
Practical
Angler
184

DEER-HAIR BLACK BEETLE

HOOK   Mustad #94833, Size 14 to 20

THREAD   Black, prewaxed 6/0

BODY   Black tying thread over deer body hair

LEGS   Surplus hair tips divided and set spentwing style with crisscross windings; trimmed to size of legs after back is finished

BACK   Deer body hair pulled forward over body and tied down in front, then set in clear lacquer

HEAD Trimmed deer hair butts
from back material

Note: You may not care for this type of legs on your beetles, but they are more durable than those made by separating three fibers on each side, as was previously the case. A "six-leg" arrangement can be made by using very thin tinted rubber string such as is often used on bass bugs, or simply heavy sewing thread tied in at the leg position and with the ends lacquered so they won't unravel. This type of leg should be secured on the underside of the body and positioned one-third body length from the hook eye.

1. Wrap the entire hook shank with tying thread to a point past the barb and tie in a bunch of deer body hair with the tips projecting forward over the eye. Secure it very tightly with thread, binding the hair down for two-thirds of the shank. The front third must be clear so the back can be tied down and a head formed. Before proceeding, give the tied-down body portion a good coat of clear lacquer.

2. Separate the hair tips into two equal bunches and set them in the position seen with crisscross windings and a little clear cement.

Terrestrial
Insects
185

Modern Fly
Dressings
for the
Practical
Angler
186

3. Grasp the long deer-hair ends that are projecting to the rear and pull them forward over the body, then tie them down on the shank in front. Pull them tight before they are secured completely, and also remove any short hairs that might not have been long enough to start with or have broken in the process.

4. Trim the surplus back hair short in front to form the head, and also trim the leg hair to size (one-third body length). Now give the beetle several good coats of clear lacquer on the head and back, as well as underneath, and it is finished.

8-4 Step 4, the finished deer-hair Black Beetle.

BLACK FEATHER BEETLE

HOOK   Mustad #94833, Size 12 to 20

THREAD   Black, prewaxed 6/0

BODY   Peacock herl palmered with black rooster hackle, trimmed top and bottom

WING   Two metallic-colored feathers from collar of ring-neck pheasant lacquered together and trimmed to shape

HEAD   Black tying thread

Terrestrial
Insects
187

Modern Fly
Dressings
for the
Practical
Angler
188

1. Wrap the entire shank with tying thread and tie in a single peacock herl and a black hackle of dry-fly quality. When the materials are tied in, wind the thread forward to a position that leaves you enough room for attaching the wing and accommodating a small head.

2. Wind the herl underbody with close turns and tie it off in front. Cut the surplus and spiral the hackle in palmer-style over it forward to the front. Take a couple of extra turns to represent the legs before tying off and cutting the surplus. Now trim away all the fibers on the underside, leaving the top and sides long.

3. Select two feathers for the wing that are large enough for the size fly being

dressed (on left in Fig. 8-7). Remove the soft fibers and fuzz on both of them, making sure that the portion to be used is the same size on both feathers (in middle). Apply some cement on both feathers and superimpose one on top of the other. Hold the exposed stems firmly with your fingers on one hand while you stroke the feathers together by repeatedly drawing them between thumb and first finger on the other hand. This will cement them together and compress the fibers a little at the same time. (Don't make them too slim, or you will ruin the silhouette.) When the cement is dry, trim the feather to length (on right in Fig. 8-7). When tied in, it should reach just barely beyond the hook bend.

Terrestrial Insects 189

8-8 Step 4, the finished Black Feather Beetle.

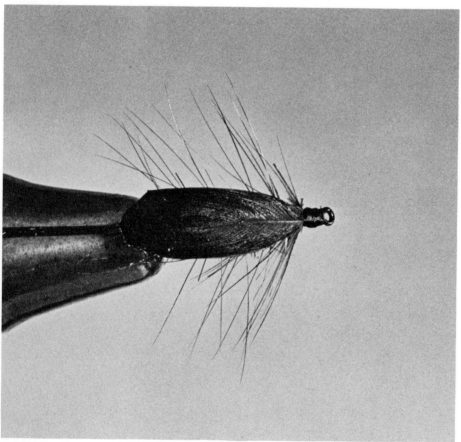

4. Divide the top hackle fibers evenly, press them down to each side, and tie in the wing so that it lies flat against the hackle fibers and herl underbody. Adjust the wing so it is parallel with the body before securing it tightly. Cut the surplus stem, wind a small head, and the Black Feather Beetle is finished.

CRICKETS AND GRASSHOPPERS (ORTHOPTERA)

When most of the important mayfly hatches have come to an end, and the warm summer days of August have slowed fishing activities on the trout stream to the point where only mini-sized artificials seem to work, it used to be customary to hand up the rod and take a swim in the large upstream pool set aside for just such occasions. It was that way until some years ago, when it was discovered that after the mayflies have come and gone, the kickers on grasshoppers and crickets have matured, giving life to the meadow and nearby flatland. Trout are like humans, they have to eat to exist, and as my friend Lefty Kreh says, "A big grasshopper—that's a lot of groceries."

The deer-hair Crickets and Hoppers have proved to be not only good fish-getters, but also very durable; they can stand the repeated punishment that so often destroys other types of flies. The size of flies you will need for a good afternoon of trout fishing is hard to predict, but in the East I have found that a Cricket dressed on a 14 hook is generally a good size. The Hopper should be slightly larger, perhaps dressed on Size 8 to 10, but what works in the East may not necessarily work out West on the fast roaring rivers. There, I suspect, they should be quite a bit larger. The best procedure is to collect some specimens when you arrive at your fishing location and match your artificials accordingly.

The method of dressing is the same for both Cricket and Hopper; the difference between them lies in the material color used.

CRICKET

HOOK	Mustad #94833, Size 10 to 14
THREAD	Black, prewaxed 6/0
BODY	Black fur dubbing
UNDERWING	Black crow wing quill section tied flat, length of hook
OVERWING	Dyed black deer-body hair, slightly longer than underwing
HEAD	Trimmed hair butts from overwing

HOPPER

HOOK	Mustad #94833, Size 8 to 12
THREAD	Yellow, prewaxed 6/0
BODY	Yellowish-tan with a touch of olive
UNDERWING	Brown mottled turkey wing quill section, length of hook
OVERWING	Natural dun-gray deer body hair, slightly longer than underwing
HEAD	Trimmed hair butts from overwing
DUBBING FORMULA	1 part yellow and 1 part tan, with enough medium-olive fur added to give it an olive cast

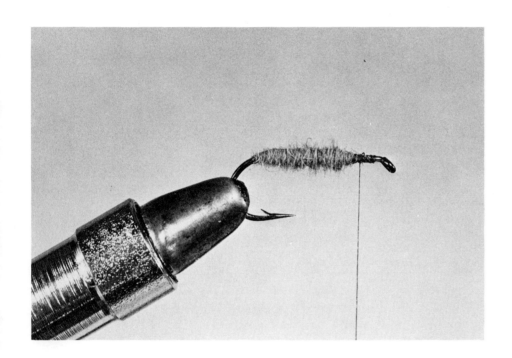

8-9 Dressing the deer-hair
Cricket or Hopper, Step 1.

Modern Fly
Dressings
for the
Practical
Angler
192

1. Dub the fur body in the usual manner by rolling the dubbing directly on the waxed tying thread, and wind it on the hook shank like an ordinary dry-fly body. Make sure it is not too skinny. Tie off the dubbing in front and cut the surplus.

There must be room enough in front to attach the wing materials and form the deer-hair head.

2. Cut a wing quill section that is wide enough to give you the proper width

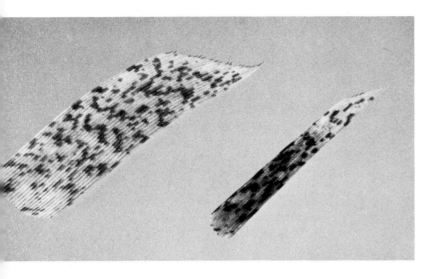

8-10 Step 2.

8-11 Step 3.

when doubled lengthwise. (Proper width is about three times the body width.) Spray it with clear adhesive (Krylon). Double the quill section lengthwise and let it dry before trimming the corners as seen at right in Fig. 8-10.

3. Lay the wing section flat and parallel over the body and tie it on in front. Cut the surplus and wind over the ends before adding a small amount of clear cement.

Terrestrial Insects
193

Modern Fly
Dressings
for the
Practical
Angler
194

4. Take a bunch of deer body hair and align the tips. Then tie them in on top of the hook. Hold the hair firmly on top; do not allow the hair to spin around the underside. At the most, they can be on each side. While still holding them very tight on top, wind your tying thread through the butt ends on top as well as under the bottom, which is allowed.

5. Trim the head flat on the bottom, then follow by trimming the top and sides as seen. There may be too much hair in the overwing, which can be trimmed away so the butts blend with the rest of the head butts.

8-13 Step 5, the finished
deer-hair Cricket or Hopper.

RED AND BLACK ANTS

At first I did not intend to include ants in this chapter because I have always felt they deserved a whole book to themselves. Having fished many streams in different parts of the country, I have yet to meet a trout fisherman who didn't treasure a little artificial ant at one time or another. The careless little creatures often venture into tree branches and grass along the stream and, like the rest of the land insects, fall or are blown into the water.

Ants can be dressed in any size you wish, but are generally best in Size 14 through 22. Since they are poor swimmers they are not tied as a dry fly, but more like a semi-dry fly that floats half submerged in the surface film. This type of "floating" can be accomplished by trimming the floating hackle top and bottom and letting the side hackle act as legs and prevent it from completely submerging. Whichever you prefer, the red or the black, the ants are dressed by the same method and only the color of the material decides the difference between them. There are times when a wet ant is more productive, and one should certainly carry both wet and dry all the time. To dress a wet ant, the body lumps must be made with tying thread instead of fur. When the two thread lumps are wound they are saturated with clear lacquer, or black enamel. The hackle on the wet dressings need not be dry-fly quality, and a hen hackle of the proper color will do nicely.

BLACK ANT

HOOK	Mustad #94833, Size 14 to 22
THREAD	Black, prewaxed 6/0
BODY	Two black fur lumps, large at the hook bend and smaller in front
HACKLE	One rusty-blue dun tied in the middle, dry-fly style, and trimmed top and bottom

RED ANT

HOOK	Mustad #94833, Size 18 to 22
THREAD	Brown, prewaxed 6/0
BODY	Two golden-brown fur lumps, large at the hook bend and smaller in front
HACKLE	One rusty-blue dun tied in the middle, dry-fly style, and trimmed top and bottom
DUBBING FORMULA	2 parts medium brown, 1 part chestnut brown, and 1 part yellow

1. Roll some fur on the tying thread and wind it on the hook shank to form the rear lump as seen.

2. Take the tying thread forward and form a smaller lump. Select a hackle and tie it in between the two lumps.

8-14 Dressing the Red Ant or
Black Ant, Step 1.

8-15 Step 2.

3. Wind the hackle in regular dry-fly style and tie it off.

4. Now trim the hackle away on top and bottom, leaving the sides long to act as legs, and the ant imitation is finished.

8-17　Step 4, the finished Red
Ant or Black Ant imitation.

9
Hellgrammite Larvae

I have often wondered if many of the well-known Woolly Worms were not meant to imitate the hellgrammite and other similar-looking creatures such as the fish fly larva and others found throughout the country. My own personal experience with the hellgrammite comes from the Potomac River in Maryland, where they are in great abundance, and consequently imitations have become very popular among those who fish for smallmouth bass. A great many anglers will search the rocky bottom of the swiftest part of the river for the larvae and use them as live bait wherever it is legal. I have used a number of good imitations for smallmouth bass on that river with good success, but they work equally well on a trout stream early in the season or for night fishing when the big fish are on the prowl. Since their natural habitat is among rocks on the stream bottom, the artificials should be weighted

to keep them down deep in the faster water.

Being the larval stage of the large dobsonfly, the hellgrammite reaches an enormous size at maturity, and specimens 2 to 3 inches long are not uncommon, although artificials are rarely dressed any larger than 1½ to 2 inches at the most. It is a vicious looking creature, predominantly flat and blackish-brown throughout its entire length. The six legs are blackish-brown and rather short in relation to the total length of the larva. The abdomen portion has lateral appendages of a dark-brownish color at each segment on either side, which in fly-tying are referred to as gills. The top of the thorax has a hard, shiny, blackish-brown shell or wing case that is almost square, and in front of the head are two heavy mandibles capable of pinching the collector's finger. If you collect hellgrammite larva for models in fly-

201

tying, I recommend that you use a net or a seine. When they are captured they can be grasped on top of the hard-shelled wing case and placed in a suitable container.

HELLGRAMMITE LARVA

BODY LENGTH	25 to 35mm
HOOK	Mustad #3665A, 6X Long, Size 2 to 6
THREAD	Black, prewaxed 6/0
TAIL	A small bunch of dyed dark-brown cock pheasant tail fiber tips, very short
UNDERBODY	A piece of .032 lead wire secured on each side of the hook shank with tying thread and clear cement
BODY	Equal parts of black and dark-brown Seal-Ex dubbing, ribbed with medium-wide black raffia or latex to form the segments
GILLS	One black and one dark-brown saddle hackle palmered wet-fly style, following front of ribbing and trimmed away top and bottom; sides trimmed to gill length
THORAX AND WING SHELL	Blackish-brown dyed rabbit fur from the back with heavy guard hairs unblended from the skin, spun in a loop and wound as a wet-fly hackle; black-and-brown-mottled turkey tail strip tied over and set in clear cement to form wing shell
MANDIBLES	Two fibers left from excess wing-shell material
LEGS	Fur and guard hairs from thorax left as is or shaped into three legs on each side with clear cement or clear silicone glue

1.   Since the body of this larva is not natural-looking if dressed on a straight hook, I start the fly by forming the shank of the desired-size hook to a slight arc and opening the hook gap a little with a pair of needlenose pliers.

2.   Wrap the entire shank with tying thread and tie in the lead wire on each side of the hook shank. The lead should be fastened tightly and kept directly alongside the shank. Use your needlenose pliers across the wire and the shank to make it even on both sides. Cover the lead wire completely with tying thread and apply some clear cement on the windings. This method of forming the underbody will give the finished body a flat effect in addition to the added weight needed when a nymph or larva must be fished deep. If no weight is needed, the body should still be flat, and the lead wire strips are replaced by two pieces of monofilament of the same diameter and attached to the shank in the same manner as described for the lead. If medium weight is needed after adding the monofilament, you can wind

Modern Fly
Dressings
for the
Practical
Angler
202

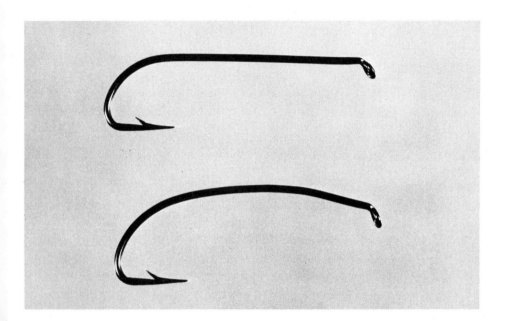

9-1 Dressing the Hellgrammite Larva, Step 1.

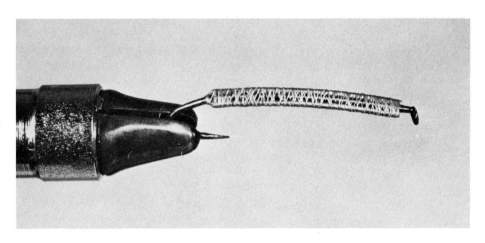

9-2 Step 2.

some .010 lead wire on a portion of the underbody and cover it with thread before the overbody is applied.

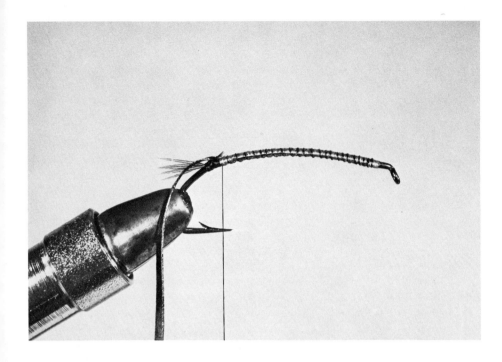

9-3   Step 3.

9-4   Step 4.

**Modern Fly
Dressings
for the
Practical
Angler
204**

3.   Take the tying thread to the shank portion directly to the rear of the under-body and tie in four to six dark-brown fiber tips. Trim away the surplus butt ends and advance the tying thread to directly on the rearmost part of the underbody

and tie in a 6-inch length of black raffia or latex on top for ribbing.

4.   Prepare the gill hackles to be tied in wet-fly style. This is done by stroking the hackles down the center spine until the

fibers stand out at a right angle. Now cut away the tip portions and trim the fibers on both sides about ½ inch up the stem, leaving only small stumps so they won't slip when tied in.

5. Tie in the hackles in the same position as the ribbing, making sure that each is securely fastened and that there is a small portion of bare stem between the first fibers and the tie-in point. This makes it easier to start the hackle when winding it.

Hellgrammite Larvae 205

9-6   Step 6.

6. Form a 4-inch spinning loop at the position where the hackles and ribbing are tied in and spin a fairly heavy dubbing mixture.

7. Hold the hackles and ribbing straight up above the hook and apply a small amount of clear cement on the under-body. Now take the first turn of dubbing closely behind the two materials, then continue to wind it tightly forward to one-third of a body length from the hook eye and tie it off. Cut the surplus dubbing and spiral the ribbing forward over the dubbed body and tie off in front.

**Modern Fly
Dressings
for the
Practical
Angler
208**

8. Wind the two hackles simultaneously in wet-fly fashion, doubling the fibers back before each turn and following in front of each turn of ribbing. Tie hackles off securely in front and cut away the surplus.

9. Trim away all the fibers close on top and bottom. Then trim the fibers on both sides to approximately one body width, to represent the gills.

9-9 Step 9.

9-10 Step 10.

10. For the wing-case shell, prepare a section of black-and-brown-mottled turkey tail that is cut wide enough to be the width of the body when doubled lengthwise. After doubling it, spray it with Krylon and let it dry.

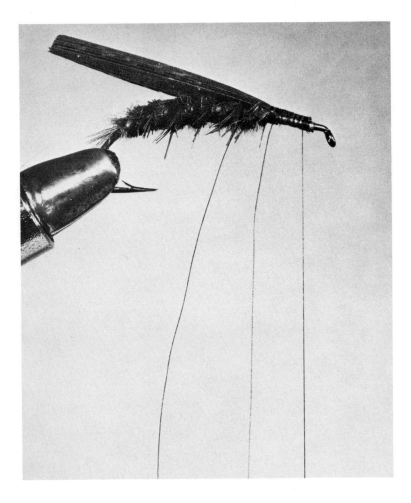

Modern Fly
Dressings
for the
Practical
Angler
210

11. Tie in the wing-shell material directly in front of the finished abdomen so that it lies flat with the butt ends projecting toward the rear, then secure it tightly on the thorax portion of the underbody. Cut the surplus ends short of the eye and take the tying thread back to directly in front of the abdomen and form a 3-inch spinning loop.

12. Cut a good bunch of fur and guard hairs that are long enough for the size legs and thorax needed. Do not disturb the natural direction of the fibers or it is not possible to form a proper fur chenille.

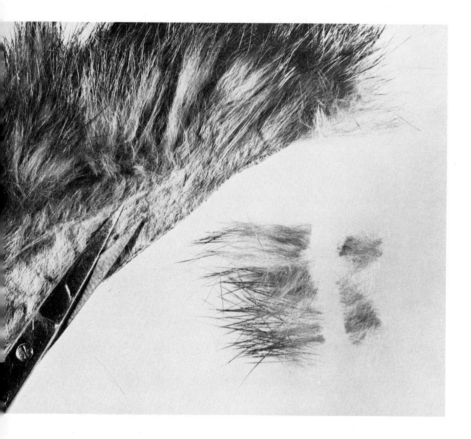

Modern Fly
Dressings
for the
Practical
Angler
212

13. Insert the fur in the loop. Note that the longest portion on one side of the loop has the tips of the guard hairs and will later form the legs.

14. Spin the fur chenille by using your heavy hackle pliers as a weight. When it is spun hold it above the hook and moisten it a little before stroking all the fur and guard hairs back so it appears to be coming out from one side of the loop.

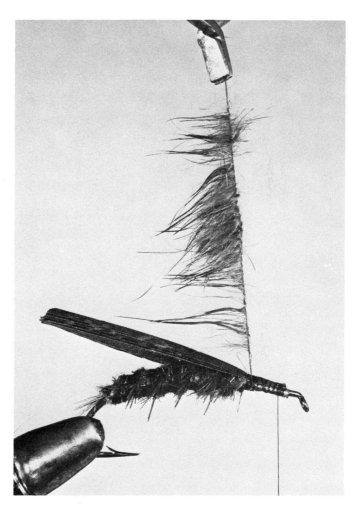

-14 Step 14.

Modern Fly
Dressings
for the
Practical
Angler
214

15. Apply some clear cement on the shank and wind the fur on the thorax portion, then tie it off in front and cut the surplus. Be sure to leave enough room in front so that the wing-shell material can be tied down and you are able to form a small head.

16. Divide the fur and guard hairs on top of the thorax and press it down on each side, then apply a small amount of clear cement in the center on top. Grasp the wing-shell material and pull it forward over the fur thorax and tie it down in front. Separate one fiber on each side of the surplus extending forward over the eye and trim away the rest. To form the mandibles, trim the remaining two fibers to length in proportion with the size fly you have dressed.

9-16　Step 16.

9-17 Step 17, the finished
Hellgrammite Larva imitation.

**Modern Fly
Dressings
for the
Practical
Angler
216**

17. The finished hellgrammite larva is now given a good coat of clear lacquer, and while still wet give it a flatter appearance by using your needlenose pliers on the abdomen portion only. Keep applying clear lacquer on the wing shell until it dries with a high shine.

Although the hellgrammite larva is shown in its finished stage in Fig. 9-17, one can shape the fur and guard hair into three legs on each side of the thorax and set them in silicone glue. This adds a little more realism in the fly and is not hard to do. This refinement is shown in Fig. 9-18.

9-18 Add a little realism, if you like, by shaping the fur and guard hairs into more clearly defined legs.

Hellgrammite
Larvae
217

SIMPLIFIED HELLGRAMMITE
AND FISH FLY LARVA

From a fly-fisher's point of view, hellgrammite and fish fly larvae are very much alike in their general appearance, so the Simplified Hell-grammite Larva is for all practical purposes the same as the Simplified Fish Fly Larva or vice versa, except that the Fish Fly is somewhat smaller and has no mandibles.

HOOK	Mustad #3665A, 6X Long, Size 2 to 6
THREAD	Black, prewaxed 6/0
TAIL GILLS	A small bunch of dyed dark-brown cock pheasant tail fiber tips, very short
UNDERBODY	A piece of .032 lead wire secured on each side of the hook shank with tying thread and clear cement
BODY	Dark-brown chenille, medium size
HACKLE	Dark-brown saddle hackle palmered, then trimmed top and bottom; remaining

fibers on each side trimmed to size for gills

The underbody is formed on the shaped hook in the exact same manner as shown in dressing the Hellgrammite Larva. Tie in the tail gill fibers in the rear, together with the hackle and a 6-inch piece of chenille. Wind the chenille forward on the under-body after applying a coat of clear cement. Go all the way to the front behind the eye with the chenille and tie it off. Cut the surplus and palmer the hackle forward and tie off in front. Trim away the excess hackle and wind a small head. Trim the hackle on the top and bottom and cut the side hackle to the appropriate gill length. To emphasize the flatness, I trim the che-nille on the top and bottom a little before applying some clear cement to the whole body, except the gills. When the cement gets a little tacky, I flatten it even more with my needlenose pliers. The finished imitation is shown in Fig. 9-19.

9-19 A simplified imitation of either the hellgrammite or the fish fly.

Index

abdomen extensions, 26, 81, 82–87, 93–98
Acroneuria (Brown Stone Fly), 179
  A. californica (Golden Stone Fly), 178–179
Adams flies, 143
adhesive, spray, 23
Adoptiva, mayflies, 55, 109–110
adults, insect, 4–7; *see also* duns; spinners
alcohol (preserving solution), 8
Alloperla (Little Green Stone Fly), 181–182
American Fly Fisher, The, 12
American Sand Sedges (caddis flies), 141
Angler's Curses (*Caenis* mayflies), 57, 106
ants, red and black, 196–199

Badger feathers, 30
Baetis (Blue Wing Olive mayfly), 56, 110–111
  B. vagans, 56
bass bugs, 16
Bay, Ken, 69
bear fur, 30
beaver fur, 30, 31
Beaverkills (*Ephemerella* mayflies), 59–60
beetles (Coleoptera), 183–190;

black, deer-hair, 184–186;
  black, feather, 28, 184, 187–190
bend shapes, hook, 10
Black Quills (*Leptophlebia* mayflies), 64, 101–102
Blades, Bill, 21, 22
blender, fur, 16
blue dun feathers, 27, 30
Blue Duns (*Adoptiva* mayflies), 55, 109–110
Blue Quills (*Adoptiva* mayflies), 55, 109–110
Blue Wing Olives (*Baetis* or *Ephemerella* mayflies), 30, 56–57, 110–111, 113–114
Boaze, Raleigh, Jr., 36, 121
body lengths, insect, 72
Bright Green Pupae (caddis flies), 141–142
Brown Drakes (*Stenonema* mayflies), 112–113
Brown Stone Flies (*Acroneuria*), 161, 179

caddis flies, 4, 11, 28, 29, 119–157; adults, 143–157; larvae, 10, 11, 121–129; nymphs, 10; pupae, 10, 23, 32, 129–143; worms, 121
Caenis mayflies, 41, 57, 88, 106

Cahills (*Stenonema* mayflies), 108
calipers, 14–15
cape feathers, 13
Capnia (Early Black Stone Fly), 180
cement, 22
chicken feathers, 26, 29–30
Cinnamon Sedges (caddis flies), 141
clippers, toenail, 17
Coachman Brown feathers, 29
Coch-y Bondhu feathers, 29
Coffin Flies (*Ephemera* mayflies), 103–104
Coleoptera Order (beetles), 183
collections, insect, 4–8, 39–40, 41, 144, 162, 191, 201–202
colors: feather, 25; marking pen, 23–24; thread, 22
Cream Variants (*Potamanthus* mayflies), 64–65, 102–103
cress bugs (crustaceans), 66
crickets (Orthoptera), 28, 191–195
crow wing quill feathers, 28
Croydon vise, 19
crustaceans, 66–67
cutters, paper, 36
Cutwing *Leptophlebias* (mayflies), 64
Cut-Wing Sulphur Duns (*Ephemerella* mayflies), 111–112

Darbee, Harry, 10, 70, 82
Darbee, Harry and Elsie, 36

Dark Blue Sedges (caddis flies), 130–138
Dark Brown Caddis Pupae, 130–138
Dark Brown Sedges (caddis flies), 130–138
Dark *Leptophlebia* Duns (mayflies), 101–102
Dark Olive Sedges (caddis flies), 141–142
Dark Red Quills (*Adoptiva* mayflies), 110
deer body hair, 26–28
delta wing pattern, 143–144, 152–153, 156
Dette, Walt, 154–155
dobsonflies, 201; larvae, *see* hellgrammites
Dressing Flies for Fresh and Salt Water (Jorgensen), 70, 82
Dr. Scholl's "Nail Clip," 17
dubbing (artificial body): fur, 31–32; roughing, 17, 45
ducks, *see* mallards; teals; wood ducks
duns (mayfly subimagos), 4, 11, 29, 31, 69–117
Dun Variants (*Isonychia* mayflies), 62–63, 71–72
dyeing fur, 33–35

Early Black Stone Flies (*Capnia*), 161, 180
Early Reddish Brown Stone Flies (*Taeniopteryx*), 179–180
elk mane, 26
emergers, mayfly, 43, 55, 57–58, 65
Epeorus fraudator (Quill Gordon mayfly), 57
    E. Pleuralis (Quill Gordon mayfly), 56, 57–58, 106–108
Ephemera guttulata (Green Drake mayfly), 35, 40–41, 59, 94, 103–104
Ephemerella mayflies, 41
    E. attenuata (Blue Wing Olive), 56, 113–114
    E. dorothea (Sulphur), 65–66, 111–112
    E. invaria, 59–60
    E. rotunda, 59–60
    E. subvaria, 59–60, 100–101
Ephemeroptera Order (mayflies), 69
Ephoron (White Fly mayfly), 55, 60–61, 88

E. leukon, 116–117
Evening Duns (*Potamanthus* mayflies), 102–103

feathers, 25–30; cutting, 15–16; measuring, 13–14
file, sharpening, 12
Fireside Angler, 36
Fishflies (*Hexagenia* mayflies), 61–62, 114–116; larvae, 11, 218–219
Fishing the Dry Fly as a Living Insect: An Unorthodox Method (Wright), 119
Flecto Varathane spray adhesive, 23
flies, dry, 11, 22, 29–31; hooks, 11
flies, wet, 22, 30, 57–59, 64–66; hooks, 10–11
floss, 25
Fly Fisherman's Bookcase Tackle Service, 19, 31, 38
Fly-Tying Materials, Their Procurement, Use and Protection (Leiser), 22
Fox, Charles K., 183
fox fur, 30
funnels, 15
fur, 30–33; bleached, 31; blending, 16, chenilles, 49; cutting, 35–36; dyed, 31, 33–35
Furnace feathers, 29–30

Gehrke's Gink (silicone), 43
General Electric Silicone Seal, 23, 82
Ginger Quills (*Stenonema* mayflies), 105–106, 108–109, 112–113
glue, silicone, 22–23
glycerine (preserving solution), 8
Golden Drakes (*Potamanthus* mayflies), 64–65, 102–103
Golden Stone Flies (*Acroneuria*), 161, 178–179
Gold-Ribbed Hare's Ears (*Stenonema* mayflies), 65
goose-wing quill feathers, 25
Gordon Quills (*Epeorus* mayflies), 57, 106–108
Grannoms (caddis flies), 130–138
grasshoppers (Orthoptera), 28, 191–195
Gray Caddis Flies, 128, 140
Gray Foxes (*Stenonema* mayflies), 30, 43, 105–106

Green Caddis larvae, 121–127
Green Drakes (*Ephemera* mayflies), 30, 59, 103–104
Grizzly feathers, 30
Grizzly Wulffs (*Hexagenia* mayflies), 114–116

hackle feathers, 13, 26, 29–30
hackle gauge, 13–14
hacksaw blades, 17
hair, aligning, 15
Hair-Wing Caddis Flies, 144–151, 156
hare mask, 32
Hare's Ears (*Stenonema* mayflies), 43, 65
hellgrammites (dobsonfly larvae), 11, 29, 201–219
Hendricksons (*Ephemerella* mayflies), 20, 59–60, 100–101
hen feathers, 26, 27, 29
Hexagenia (Michigan Caddis mayfly), 35, 41, 61–62, 94
    H. limbata, 114–116
Hille, E., 38
hooks, 9–12; ordering, 11; sizes, 12
Howard, Herb, 22
How to Tie Freshwater Flies (Bay), 69

imagos, insect, *see* spinners
insects: anatomy, 70, 72, 120, 159–162, 201; behavior, 119; collecting, 4–7, 39, 41, 144, 162, 191, 201–202; life cycles, 4; terrestrial, 183–199; *see also* duns; emergers; larvae; nymphs; pupae; spinners
Iron mayflies, 40
Iron Blue Duns (*Epeorus* mayflies), 106–108
Iron Duns (*Epeorus* mayflies), 57, 106–108
irresistible dry fly, 96
Isonychia mayflies, 25–26, 62–64, 70, 71–72, 82–88, 90–93; cutwing, 76–80; hairwing, 73–75, 76–77; Realistic, 29
    I. bicolor, 62–63, 71–72
    I. sadleri, 62–63, 71–72
Isoperla (Little Yellow Stone Fly), 181

Jack's Tackle, 38

Index
222

Kreh, Lefty, 191
Krylon Crystal Clear Spray adhesive, 23

lacquer, clear, 22
Lady Beaverkills (*Ephemerella* mayflies), 100–101
Large Black Stone Flies (*Pteronarcys*), 161, 178
Large Reddish Brown Caddis Pupae, 142
Large Red Sedges (caddis flies), 142
Large Western Salmon Flies (*Pteronarcys* stone flies), 176–177
larvae, insect, 4–5; caddis, 10, 11, 121–129; dobsonfly, *see* hellgrammites; fishfly, 11, 218–219
latex, 36; pupae, 139; wing cases, 53–54
Leadwing Coachmen (*Isonychia* mayflies), 62–64, 71–72
lead wire, 24–25
leg size, insect, 35
Leiser, Eric, 22, 30, 31, 129
Leptophlebia mayflies, 29, 41
    L. cupida (Black Quill), 64, 101–102

Light Cahills (*Stenonema* mayflies), 43, 108–109, 143
Lilly's Fly Shop, 38
Limerick bends, hook, 10
Little Blue Mayflies (*Adoptiva*), 55, 109–110
Little Blue-Winged Baetis Duns (*Baetis* mayflies), 110–111
Little Brown Sedges (caddis flies), 139–140
Little Green Stone Flies (*Alloperla*), 161, 181–182
Little Marryatts (*Ephemerella* mayflies), 65–66, 111–112
Little Olive Cutwings (*Ephemerella* mayflies), 56
Little Sulphur Duns (*Ephemerella* mayflies), 111–112
Little Yellow Stone Flies (*Isoperla*), 161, 181

mallard feathers, 26, 28, 29
Marasco, Tony, 16
March Browns (*Stenonema* mayflies), 28, 30, 112–113

Marinaro, Vince, 183
marking pens, waterproof felt tip, 23–24, 25, 36
mayflies, 4, 22–23, 119–121; anatomy, 70, 72, 159; duns, 4, 11, 29, 31, 69–117; emergers, 43, 55, 57–58, 65; nymphs, 10, 29, 32, 39–67; spinners, 4, 11, 26, 31, 69–117
measuring scale cards, 13, 14, 72, 77
Medium Blue-Winged Olives (*Ephemerella* mayflies), 113–114
Medium Brown Pupae (caddis flies), 139–140
Medium Brown Sedges (caddis flies), 139–140
Michigan Caddises (*Hexagenia* mayflies), 61–62, 114–116
mink fur, 28, 30, 31, 32
minnows, muddler, 96
monofilament, 25
moose mane, 26
moths, 144
Multi-Variants (*Ephemera* mayflies), 59
Mustad hooks, 10–12

nail polish, 22, 23, 82
neck hackles, chicken, 21, 26, 29–30; photodyed, 30
nets: aquarium, 5; butterfly, 5
nylon: floss, 25; thread, 22
nymph hooks, 10–11
nymphs, insect, 4–5, 22–32; caddis, 10; mayfly, 10, 29, 30, 39–67; miniature, 11; stone fly, 10, 25, 29, 32, 159–182
Nymphs: A Complete Guide to Naturals and Their Imitations (Schwiebert), 119

opossum fur, 30, 36; Australian, 32
Olive Caddis larvae, 128
Orange Caddis larvae, 128
Orothoptera Order (crickets and grasshoppers), 191
ostrich, mini-, herl feathers, 25

Pale Brown Pupae (caddis flies), 140
Pale Evening Duns (*Ephemerella* mayflies), 65–66, 111–112
Pale Olive Pupae (caddis flies), 142
parachute duns, 11

parachute hackle, 30, 70
Paraleptophlebia adoptiva (Little Blue mayfly), 55, 109–110
peacock herl feathers, 25
Perla stone flies, 161, 162–175, 178
    P. capitata, 162, 178, 179
pheasants, cock, feathers, 25, 26, 29; ring neck, 28
pliers: hackle, 132; needlenose, 163
Plymouth Rock chickens, 30
Potamanthus Cutwings (mayflies), 64–65
    P. distinctus (Golden Drake), 64–65, 102–103
preserving solutions, 7–8
pronotum (upper thorax), 174–175
Pteronarcys californica (Western Salmon stone fly), 176–178
    P. dorsata (Large Black stone fly), 178
pupae, 23; caddis, 10, 23, 32, 129–143

Quill Gordons (*Epeorus pleuralis* mayflies), 56–58, 106–108, 143
quill section equalizer, 15–16

rabbit fur, 30, 32, 36
raffia, 202
razor blades, 21, 36
Realistics (lifelike mayflies), 29, 80–88, 100–103, 108–111, 114, 115
Reddish Brown Stone Flies (*Taeniopteryx*), 161, 179–180
Red Quills (Ephemerella mayflies), 59–60, 100–101
Rit Dye, 33
rooster nick, 21
rubber string, 185

saddles, rooster, 29–30
salmon hooks, 10, 156
Sand Sedges (caddis flies), 141
Schwiebert, Ernest, 119
scissors, 12, 13
scud, yellow (crustaceans), 66–67
Seal-Ex, 32
seal fur, 31
sedges, *see* caddis flies
seines, 5
shank lengths, hook, 9, 12
sharpening stone, 12

shrimp, freshwater (crustaceans), 66–67
silicone: flotant, 43; glue, 22–23
silk: floss, 25; thread, 22
Small Dun Variants (Ephemerella mayflies), 56, 113–114
Solomon, Larry, 143, 157
sowbugs (crustaceans), 66
spade hackles, 26
Speckled Sedges (caddis flies), 140
spinners (mayfly imagos), 4, 11, 26, 31, 69–117
Spotted Sedges (caddis flies), 140
spray adhesive, 23
Sproat bends, hook, 10
Stenonema mayflies, 28, 40, 43–61, 65
  S. candense (Light Cahill), 43, 108–109
  S. fuscum (Gray Fox), 43, 105–106
  S. ithaca (Cahill), 108–109
  S. vicarium (March Brown), 43, 112–113
stone flies, 4, 119–121; anatomy, 159–162; nymphs, 10, 25, 29, 32, 159–182
subimagos, see duns
Sulphurs (Ephemerella mayflies), 65–66
suppliers, 11, 19, 31, 36–38

Taeniopteryx (Early Reddish Brown stone fly), 179–180
tails, insect, 25–26; lengths, 72
teal feathers, 26, 28, 29
thread, 22
thread, sewing, 185
tinsel tags, gold, 64
Tiny White-Winged Duns (Caenis mayflies), 57, 106
tools, fly-tying, 12–19
Trichoptera Order (caddis flies), 119, 144
Tricotythodes mayflies, 57, 88, 106
Trimmer, Ross, 183
Trout Magazine, 17
turkey feathers, 28, 29
tweezers, 7
tying kit, portable, 17–19

Veniard, E., Ltd., 38
vinegar, 8, 33
vise, 12–13, 19

wax, 22
weights, 24–25
Western Caperers (caddis flies), 141–142
Western Salmon Flies (stone flies), 161, 176–177

Whirling Duns (Peptophlebia mayflies), 64, 101–102
White Caddis Flies, 128
White Flies (Ephoron mayflies), 60–61, 116–117
White-Gloved Howdies (Isonychia mayflies), 62–63, 71–72
White Millers (Ephoron mayflies), 60–61, 116–117
White-Winged Ephoron Duns (mayflies), 116–117
White Wulffs (Ephemera mayflies), 104
wing cutters, 17
wings, insect, 26–28; attaching, 78–80; cutting, 77–78; delta, 143–144, 152–153, 156; latex, 53–54; lengths, 72
woodchuck fur, 30
wood duck feathers, 25, 26, 28
wool, chopping, 16
wool, crewel, 25, 139
Wright, Leonard W., Jr., 119

X-Acto knife, 15, 36
X-Acto saw, 16–17

Yellow Caddis Larvae, 128–129